Creating ChatGPT Apps with JavaScript

A Hands-on Guide for AI Applications with OpenAI APIs

Bruce Hopkins Jr.
Bruce Hopkins Sr.

Apress®

Creating ChatGPT Apps with JavaScript: A Hands-on Guide for AI Applications with OpenAI APIs

Bruce Hopkins Jr.
Brandon, FL, USA

Bruce Hopkins Sr.
Beaverton, OR, USA

ISBN-13 (pbk): 979-8-8688-1220-0
https://doi.org/10.1007/979-8-8688-1221-7

ISBN-13 (electronic): 979-8-8688-1221-7

Managing Director, Apress Media LLC: Welmoed Spahr
Acquisitions Editor: Melissa Duffy
Development Editor: James Markham
Editorial Assistant: Gryffin Winkler

Cover designed by eStudioCalamar

Distributed to the book trade worldwide by Springer Science+Business Media New York, 1 New York Plaza, Suite 4600, New York, NY 10004-1562, USA. Phone 1-800-SPRINGER, fax (201) 348-4505, e-mail orders-ny@springer-sbm.com, or visit www.springeronline.com. Apress Media, LLC is a California LLC and the sole member (owner) is Springer Science + Business Media Finance Inc (SSBM Finance Inc). SSBM Finance Inc is a **Delaware** corporation.

For information on translations, please e-mail booktranslations@springernature.com; for reprint, paperback, or audio rights, please e-mail bookpermissions@springernature.com.

Apress titles may be purchased in bulk for academic, corporate, or promotional use. eBook versions and licenses are also available for most titles. For more information, reference our Print and eBook Bulk Sales web page at http://www.apress.com/bulk-sales.

Any source code or other supplementary material referenced by the author in this book is available to readers on GitHub. For more detailed information, please visit https://www.apress.com/gp/services/source-code.

If disposing of this product, please recycle the paper

Table of Contents

About the Authors

Bruce Hopkins Jr. works as a senior software developer and consultant for a fast-growing startup specializing in creating cutting-edge B2B and B2C applications based in Dallas, Texas. With years of experience as a full-stack developer, Bruce Jr. is passionate about building robust, user-friendly software applications and services using his favorite languages, JavaScript and TypeScript. He has hands-on experience with AI toolsets like OpenAI ChatGPT and Meta Llama and has used them in both research and professional AI-powered solutions. Beyond his professional expertise, Bruce actively contributes to the open source community, dedicating countless hours to fixing bugs, enhancing projects, and improving tools like the very popular Microsoft VS Code. When he's not coding, you might find him mentoring junior developers, attending tech meetups, or staying up to date with the latest trends in artificial intelligence and software development.

Bruce Hopkins Sr. has been an author and technical writer with more than 20 years of experience writing articles and blogs for some of the world's leading technology companies, including Intel, IBM, Oracle, and the official Linux Magazine. Beyond technical writing, Bruce Sr. has been at the forefront of research in natural language processing (NLP) and artificial intelligence (AI), with a particular focus on speech recognition and chatbot technologies. His innovative contributions in these fields have earned him the prestigious title of Intel Innovator for AI and IoT. Bruce's passion for technology extends beyond writing – he actively explores emerging trends in AI, bridging the gap between complex technical concepts and practical, real-world applications. His work not only informs but also inspires the next generation of tech professionals and innovators. With a commitment to advancing the understanding and adoption of AI, Bruce remains a thought leader in this rapidly evolving industry.

About the Technical Reviewer

Satej Kumar Sahu works in the role of Principal Data Engineer at Zalando SE, with 14 years of experience in the industry. He is passionate about technology, people, and nature. He has worked with organizations such as Boeing, Adidas, and Honeywell, specializing in software, architecture, big data, and machine learning use cases. With a strong track record of architecting scalable and efficient systems, Satej has successfully delivered software, data-driven, and ML applied solutions. He believes that through technology and conscientious decision-making, each of us has the power to make this world a better place. In his free time, he can be found reading books, playing basketball, and having fun with friends and family.

CHAPTER 1

Introducing ChatGPT for JavaScript Developers

Who Is This Book For?

First of all, this book is for JavaScript developers who don't have any training or experience in artificial intelligence, natural language processing, machine learning, or deep learning. You may have heard of the term "language model," but I'm going to assume that it's NOT a term that you use every day.

Secondly, you might be familiar with (or have tried) ChatGPT, but you don't *quite* understand how everything works "under the hood" and you're not sure how to get started in order to use JavaScript and ChatGPT programmatically together to "AI enable" your own applications and services.

© Bruce Hopkins Jr., Bruce Hopkins Sr. 2025
B. Hopkins Jr. and B. Hopkins Sr., *Creating ChatGPT Apps with JavaScript*,
https://doi.org/10.1007/979-8-8688-1221-7_1

> **Note**   Although ChatGPT is a household name, OpenAI, the company behind it, lacks broad recognition and isn't as widely recognized. So, although this book is about how to use ChatGPT programmatically within your JavaScript apps, the APIs that we will be using are officially the OpenAI REST APIs. Therefore, we'll be using the term "ChatGPT API" and "OpenAI API" synonymously.

Chapter Overview

In this chapter, we're going to dive right in and explain a few terms that you might not be familiar with, and then go straight to the ChatGPT Playground. The Playground is essentially a web interface for developers that's built on top of ChatGPT REST API. So, once you're familiar with the Playground, the calls and responses from the ChatGPT API will feel like second nature to you.

Download the Code Now!

This book is filled with tons of examples and example code, so why bother typing everything yourself? Below is the URL to the GitHub repo to access the source code.

https://github.com/JavaScriptChatGPT/

So, What Exactly Is ChatGPT and Why Do I Need to Use the OpenAI APIs?

Simply stated, ChatGPT is a group of **language models** (which are the result of training deep learning algorithms) developed by OpenAI that is capable of generating human-like text responses based on given prompts. So what's a prompt? A prompt is simply the input text that you give to ChatGPT. So let's kick things off by giving ChatGPT a prompt to ask how well it's familiar with JavaScript design patterns. Head over to the chatgpt. com website, and enter the following prompt from Listing 1-1.

Listing 1-1. PROMPT. A Simple Prompt with ChatGPT About JavaScript Design Patterns

```
Describe 3 commonly used design patterns used by JavaScript
developers and why those patterns are important
```

If you've had the opportunity to work at a company using JavaScript professionally, then you've probably received a question very similar to the prompt above in an interview. Listing 1-2 is ChatGPT's response.

Listing 1-2. RESPONSE. ChatGPT's Response to the Prompt in Listing 1-1

```
JavaScript developers commonly use design patterns to manage
code complexity and enhance code maintainability, readability,
and scalability. Here are three widely used design patterns in
JavaScript:
```

1. Module Pattern

The Module pattern is used to encapsulate a group of related methods or variables into a single unit or module, shielding parts from the global scope. This pattern helps in:

- Reducing Namespace Pollution: By minimizing the use of global variables, this pattern helps avoid namespace pollution.

- Encapsulation: It enables better encapsulation and protects the module's states and behaviors from outside interference.

- Code Organization: It promotes organizational and structural clarity by dividing responsibilities across distinct modules.

2. Observer Pattern

The Observer pattern is a software design pattern in which an object, called the subject, maintains a list of its dependents, called observers, and notifies them automatically of any state changes, usually by calling one of their methods. This pattern is crucial for

- Decoupling: It decouples the objects that invoke the behavior from the objects that perform the behavior, leading to a cleaner and more flexible architecture.

- Event Handling: It's widely used in the handling of user interface events and other scenarios where certain objects need to be notified of changes occurring in other objects.

- Reactive Programming: Facilitates a reactive programming approach where changes propagate through the system in response to events.

3. Singleton Pattern
The Singleton pattern ensures that a class has only one
instance and provides a global point of access to it. This
pattern is widely used for

- Controlled Access: It provides controlled access to a
  single instance, which can be useful for managing shared
  resources or configurations.

- Initialization Guarantee: Ensures that a class is
  instantiated once and only once, which can be critical for
  many shared resources.

- Lazy Initialization: Often implemented with lazy
  initialization, saving system resources by postponing the
  creation of the instance until it's needed.

Not bad, huh? ChatGPT was not only able to provide a list of common design patterns used by JavaScript developers, but also explain valid reasons on why they are important – all done in Natural Language.

So, at the end of the day, what does this mean for JavaScript developers? Well, it's actually a big deal. That's because developers are now able to create applications that can have some type of "understanding" of text in Natural Language. Before the advent of AI tools like ChatGPT, developers typically had to create regular expressions (also called "regex") in order to perform rudimentary character and String pattern matching within a body of text. However, pattern matching and Natural Language Understanding are two totally different things.

Regex vs. ChatGPT – Fight!

Note   If you already know that a regular expression can't perform Natural Language Understanding or sentiment analysis, then feel free to skip this section.

I'm thoroughly convinced that every programmer somewhere in their lifetime has met *somebody* who happens to be an expert in writing regular expressions. Regular expressions are great because they serve the purpose of being able to parse large amounts of text in order to find patterns within the text programmatically.

However, one of the biggest downsides to regular expressions is that once they have been written, they are extremely difficult to read (in my opinion, even by the developer who originally wrote it).

So let's see how regex holds up against ChatGPT, which has Natural Language Processing (NLP) and Natural Language Understanding (NLU) capabilities.

Listing 1-3 is a story of an impractically sad situation. However, it drives home the point that although regular expressions can be used to find words and phrases within a body of text, it can't be used to provide any type of NLU.

Listing 1-3. Sadstory.txt – A Sad Story About a Kid Who Didn't Eat Ice Cream

```
In the city of Buttersville, United States, on Milkmaid street,
there's a group of three friends: Marion Yogurt, Janelle de
Queso, and Steve Cheeseworth III. On a hot summer's day, they
heard the music from an ice cream truck and decided to buy
something to eat.
```

```
Marion likes strawberries, Janelle prefers chocolate, and Steve
is lactose intolerant. That day, only two kids ate ice cream,
and one of them bought a bottle of room-temperature water. The
ice cream truck was fully stocked with the typical flavors of
ice cream.
```

Analysis Question #1: Who Didn't Get Any Ice Cream and Why?

Now let's analyze this for a bit and ask some questions among ourselves. First of all, who didn't get any ice cream and why? The obvious answer is that Steve did not get any ice cream because of his lactose intolerance. However, since the story did not directly say that Steve did not buy ice cream, there's no way for a regular expression to match a text pattern in the story.

The regular expression could look for keywords such as "didn't have," "no ice cream," or the names of the kids. However, it would only be able to provide a response based on the presence of these patterns. For example, if the regular expression matches the pattern "didn't have" or "no ice cream" with Steve's name, it could show you the result of the text pattern. However, it certainly wouldn't be able to explain why Steve was the one who didn't have ice cream or provide any context-specific reasoning.

Now, let's provide the same story to ChatGPT, and ask the question, "Who didn't get any ice cream?" Listing 1-4, located below, takes our question and the story above and puts both together as a prompt.

Listing 1-4. PROMPT. The Sad Story Put Into a Prompt

```
Using the information in the story below, who didn't get any
ice cream and why?
###
In the city of Buttersville, United States, on Milkmaid street,
there's a group of three friends: Marion Yogurt, Janelle de
Queso, and Steve Cheeseworth III. On a hot summer's day, they
heard the music from an ice cream truck, and decided to buy
something to eat.

Marion likes strawberries, Janelle prefers chocolate, and Steve
is lactose intolerant. That day, only two kids ate ice cream,
and one of them bought a bottle of room-temperature water. The
ice cream truck was fully stocked with the typical flavors of
ice cream.
```

Notice how it is a best practice to provide some type of separation, in this case, "###", when creating a prompt (like the one above) where you have both instructions and data together. Later on, when we start using either the Playground or JavaScript to programmatically invoke the ChatGPT API, you'll see that there's a much better way to provide that separation.

So, after sending the prompt, ChatGPT will provide you an answer like shown in Listing 1-5:

Listing 1-5. RESPONSE. ChatGPT's Answer to Analysis Question #1

```
Based on the given information, Steve is lactose intolerant and
therefore cannot eat ice cream. Therefore, Steve is the one who
didn't get any ice cream.
```

As you can see, ChatGPT can utilize NLP and NLU, and therefore it can understand (artificially intelligently, that is) the context of the scenario. It can interpret the relationships between the kids, their preferences, and Steve's lactose intolerance. It is able to understand that the last names of the children, the street name, and the city name are the names of dairy products, but are obviously irrelevant to the question at hand.

Analysis Question #2: Which Kid Was Probably Left Sad?

Now to further prove the point that a regular expression is unable to provide any type of NLP or NLU, now let's use a new term called **sentiment analysis**. Therefore, after the ice cream truck drove away, which kid was left sad?

Since the story had no mention of any of the children's feelings or emotions, there is no text pattern that would allow any regular expression to return a match.

However, if you posed the same question to ChatGPT, it will return a response like shown in Listing 1-6:

Listing 1-6. RESPONSE. ChatGPT's Answer to Analysis Question #2

Since Steve is lactose intolerant and cannot eat ice cream, he would be the kid left sad because he couldn't enjoy the ice cream like Marion and Janelle.

Therefore, ChatGPT is able to comprehend the scenario, reason through the information, and provide a correct answer along with an explanation for that answer.

Let's Unlearn Some Words in Order to Learn More About the ChatGPT API

First of all, before you get started working with the ChatGPT and OpenAI APIs, there are few words and terms that you should be familiar with first; otherwise, things won't exactly make sense. So let's make sure that we're all clear on the definition of Models, Prompts, Tokens, and Temperature when using ChatGPT programmatically.

Models. Models? Models!!!

As a JavaScript developer, when you hear the term "model," you may immediately think of the representation of real-world entities in your JavaScript app, right? For example, think of the term, "object model." Additionally, if you're ever worked with any type of database before, then the term "model" may ALSO conjure into your mind the idea of the representation of data and their relationships in your database. For example, think of the term, "data model."

However, when working with the ChatGPT APIs (and artificial intelligence in general, for that matter) you need to forget both of those definitions, because they don't apply. In the realm of artificial intelligence, a "model" is a pre-trained **neural network**.

Remember, as I mentioned earlier, you won't need a PhD in Machine Learning in order to read this book. So what's a neural network? Simply stated, a neural network is a fundamental component of artificial intelligence systems, because they are designed to simulate the way the human brain works by using interconnected layers of artificial neurons to process and analyze data. These networks can be trained on vast amounts of data to learn patterns, relationships, and to make predictions.

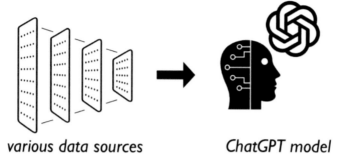

various data sources   ChatGPT model

Figure 1-1. *An AI Model Is Trained on Vast Amounts of Data*

In the context of AI, a "pre-trained model" refers to a neural network that has been trained on a specific task or dataset before being made available for use by developers. This training process involves exposing the model to large amounts of labeled and categorized (also called, "annotated") data and adjusting its internal parameters to optimize its performance on the given task.

Let's look at some of the models provided by OpenAI for developers to use to AI-enable their applications.

o1	The o1 series of large language models is trained through reinforcement learning to handle complex reasoning tasks. o1 models engage in deep thought before answering, generating a lengthy internal chain of reasoning prior to responding to the user. These models take a significantly longer time to generate a response than other models.
	Some o1 available models are
	• o1
	• o1-mini

(*continued*)

GPT-4	GPT-4 is one of the latest generation of OpenAI's GPT set of models. GPT stands for Generative Pre-trained Transformer, and these models have been trained to understand natural language as well as multiple programming languages. The GPT-4 models take text and images as inputs as the prompt and provide text as the output. Some of the GPT-4 models available are • gpt-4o • gpt-4o-mini • gpt-4o-realtime • gpt-4o-audio
GPT-3.5	GPT-3.x is the previous generation of OpenAI's GPT set of models. The original ChatGPT released to the public in November 2022 used GPT 3. Some of the GPT-3 models available are • gpt-3.5-turbo • gpt-3.5-turbo-16k
DALL·E	The DALL·E model can generate and edit images given a natural language prompt. Later in this book in Chapter 5, we're going to have some fun with the DALL·E model to visualize the conversation of what is being discussed in your favorite podcast episode. Some of the DALL·E models available are • dall-e-3 • dall-e-2

(continued)

TTS	The TTS model takes text and converts it to audio with surprisingly good results. In most cases, the audio is almost indistinguishable from a human voice.
	Some of the TTS models available are
	<ul><li>tts-1</li><li>tts-1-hd</li></ul>
Whisper	Simply stated, the Whisper model converts audio into text.
	In this book, we're going to use the Whisper model to search for text in a podcast episode.
Embeddings	The Embeddings model can convert large amounts of text into a numerical representation of how the Strings in the text are related. So how is that useful? Embeddings allows developers to do specific tasks using custom datasets. Yes, this means that you can train the embeddings model on specific data that is relevant to your application. This allows you to do operations such as
	<ul><li>Searching within your own body of text</li><li>Clustering data so that strings of text are grouped by their similarity</li><li>Getting recommendations (where items with related text strings are recommended)</li><li>Detecting anomalies (where outliers with little relatedness are identified)</li><li>Measuring diversity (where similarity distributions are analyzed)</li><li>Classifying data (where text strings are classified by their most similar label)</li></ul>

(*continued*)

13

Moderation	The moderation models are fine-tuned models that can detect whether text may be sensitive or unsafe. These models can analyze text content and classify it according to the following categories:

- Hate
- Hate/threatening
- Harassment
- Harassment/threatening
- Self-harm
- Self-harm/intent
- Self-harm/instructions
- Sexual
- Sexual/minors
- Violence
- Violence/graphic

The moderation models available are

- text-moderation-latest
- text-moderation-stable

Legacy and Deprecated	Since the debut of ChatGPT, OpenAI has continued to support their older AI models, but they have been labeled as "legacy" or "deprecated" models. These models continue to exist; however, they have released other models that are more accurate, faster, and cheaper to use.

Note   This is by no means an exhaustive list of models available for developers provided by OpenAI! As newer models are released, the older models will be marked as legacy or deprecated. Therefore, it's important to stay up to date by checking the list of available models on the OpenAI documentation list of models:

`https://platform.openai.com/docs/models`

When We Talk About Tokens, Don't Think About Access Tokens

When using a third-party API, such as an external REST service, you might think of a "token" in the same sense as an access token, which is typically a UUID that allows you to identify yourself and maintain a session with the service. Well, forget that definition for now. Instead, when using the OpenAI APIs, a **token** is a chunk of a text that is approximately 4 characters long. That's it – nothing else special.

So if a token is approximately a 4-character chunk of text, then why do we care about it?

When working with the OpenAI textual models, developers need to be aware of token limitations, because they impact the cost and performance of API calls. For example, the gpt-4o and o1 models both support 128,000 tokens (which is approximately the size of a 300-page novel) that can go in your prompt. These input tokens are also called the **context window**. In contrast, the maximum output tokens for gpt-4o is 16,384, while the maximum output tokens for the o1 model is 32,768.

As a result, developers need to take into account the length of the prompts as inputs and outputs to the models, ensuring that they fit within the model's token constraints.

Table 1-1 provides a list of some of the most current models with the token limitations and their pricing.

Table 1-1. *List of Models with Their Token Limitations and the Cost per Token*

Model	Context Window	Cost of Token Input	Cost of Token Output
gpt-4o	128,000	$2.50 / 1M tokens	$10.00 / 1M tokens
gpt-4o-mini	128,000	$0.15 / 1M tokens	$0.60 / 1M tokens
o1	128,000	$15.00 / 1M tokens	$60.00 / 1M tokens
o1-mini	128,000	$3.00 / 1M tokens	$12.00 / 1M tokens

Temperature Is All About Creativity

Of course, ChatGPT isn't sentient, so it's incapable of thinking as we humans do. However, by adjusting the **temperature** setting in your prompts to the ChatGPT API, you can enable the responses to be more creative. Being aware of what it understands is crucial if you want to make best use of its potential.

Figure 1-2. *Modify the Temperature in Order to Get More (or Less) Creative Responses*

Now it's time to take the concepts that we've learned so far and start to put them to good use! However, we need to do first things first, and therefore you will need to have a developer account with OpenAI and create an API key.

Head over to the following URL to create your dev account and API key:

```
https://platform.openai.com/account/api-keys
```

As you can see from the image below, you can name your API key anything that you want.

Getting Started with the OpenAI Playground

Now it's time to take the concepts that we've learned so far and start to put them to good use! However, we need to do first things first, and therefore you will need to have a developer account with OpenAI and create an API key.

Head over to the following URL to create your dev account and API key:

https://platform.openai.com/account/api-keys

As you can see from Figure 1-3, you can name your API key anything that you want.

Figure 1-3. *Before You Can Access the Playground or Make API Calls, You Need to Have an API Key*

You should be aware that as a requirement to create an API key, you will need to provide to OpenAI a credit card so that you can be billed for usage of their models.

Now that you've got your API key, let's go straight to the Chat Playground at the following URL:

`https://platform.openai.com/playground`

Figure 1-4 depicts the Chat Playground, with certain parts numbered so that they can be easily identified.

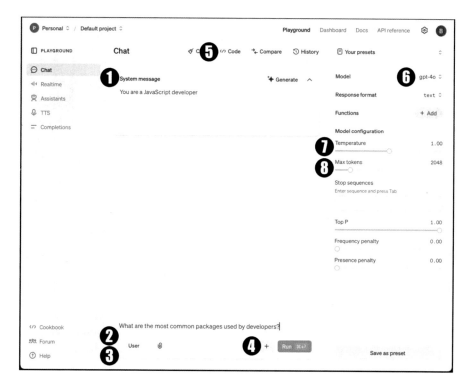

Figure 1-4. *The Chat Playground Can Be a Little Daunting at First Glance*

1. System Message

As you can see, the user interface for the Chat Playground is vastly more complex than the ChatGPT website that everyone else uses. So let's talk about the **System Message** field (see Figure 1-4, item 1).

In our opinion, ChatGPT can be described as, "a vastly powerful form of artificial intelligence… with amnesia." Therefore, when you're using ChatGPT programmatically, you need to inform the system who it is in the conversation!

Figure 1-5, shown below, gives you a glimpse of the thousands of different roles that ChatGPT can play in a conversation.

System: " **You are a...** "

"economist"   "blogger"   "15th century poet"   "Chef"

Figure 1-5. *The System Message Field in the Chat Playground Allows You to Set the Role That ChatGPT Will Play in the Conversation*

2. User

The **User** field (Figure 1-4, item 2) in the Chat Playground is where you type your prompt to ChatGPT, which can be anything that you want, for example, "What are the most common packages used by developers?"

3. Assistant (Optional)

When you initially load the Chat Playground, the **Assistant** field (Figure 1-4, item 3) is not visible. In order to make it appear, you need to do the following:

- Type in a User message.

- Click the "+" button to add the message to the conversation.

- Click the User button, to toggle the message type from "User" to "Assistant."

Now, you may be asking yourself, "Why is this field needed at all?" Well, that's a fine question. If you want ChatGPT to remember something that it has already told you in a previous conversation, then you need to type into the **Assistant** field anything that it has already told you that you think is relevant in order to continue with the conversation. Remember, it is a vastly powerful AI, but it has amnesia!

4. + (Optional)

The "**+**" button (Figure 1-4, item 4) is where you'd click in order to add either an **Assistant** message to the conversation or another **User** message. Now, you may ask, "What's the point of adding yet another User message to the conversation, when I can type what I want in the original User field above?" Good question.

If you wanted to separate your commands from your data, then you would use a separate **User** message for that.

Do you remember in Listing 1-4 earlier in this chapter, where we had to use the "###" to separate the command to ChatGPT from the data that we wanted it to analyze? Well, this is now no longer needed because the command would be the first **User** message, and the data would be the second **User** message.

5. Code (Optional)

After you have submitted your prompt using the Playground, you can click the **Code** button (Figure 1-4, item 5) in order to see the code necessary to send the same prompt using any of the languages that they support.

6. Model (Optional)

Earlier in this chapter, we talked about the various models that are available for developers. Click the model field in order to see a list of models that are available.

You may also see that some models have a month and day associated with their name, which is simply a snapshot of that model. Programmatically selecting a snapshot enables developers to have some sort of predictability in the responses that they will receive from ChatGPT, because the current models are always updated.

7. Temperature (Optional)

As noted earlier in this chapter, the temperature selector ranges between 0 and 2 and allows you to select the "randomness" of the response.

8. Max Tokens (Optional)

Do you remember the discussion earlier in this chapter about tokens? By selecting anything in the range for this item, you can adjust the number of tokens (which directly affects the number of words) in the response.

Try It Now! Experimenting with the "System" Role

Now that we're familiar with several of the features of the Chat Playground, let's send our first prompt using the settings discussed above. Listings 1-7 and 1-8 below use the same prompt asking ChatGPT to give a few paragraphs on telemedicine, but the role of the system is vastly different from each other.

Listing 1-7. PROMPT. The Pros and Cons of Telemedicine as a Researcher

```
System: You are a strictly factual researcher
User: Write 3 paragraphs on pros and cons of telemedicine
```

Listing 1-8. PROMPT. The Pros and Cons of Telemedicine as an Opinionated Health Blogger

System: You are a highly opinionated health blogger who always has stories with first hand experience
User: Write 3 paragraphs on pros and cons of telemedicine

You are encouraged to try these two prompts yourself and see what the responses are. Adjust the settings for the temperature and token length to get familiar with how those parameters affect the outcome.

Conclusion

You just learned more about how ChatGPT can be used by developers. We covered some of the basics of the Chat Playground, which is a web interface for developers to interact with the ChatGPT API.

We talked about how to set the system, user, and assistant roles in the Chat Playground and how to adjust settings such as the temperature and maximum length of output.

You learned about some of the parameters and terminology necessary to use the Chat Playground, such as the model, the temperature, and tokens. Getting familiar with the parameters of the Chat Playground is essential to knowing how to use the REST API since the Playground is a subset of capabilities offered by the REST API.

In the next chapter, we'll see how to use ChatGPT as your "pair programmer" and create a productivity app that gives us weather and arrival time to work.

CHAPTER 2

Using ChatGPT As Your JavaScript Pair-Programmer

I'm a big fan of some of the practices of XP (eXtreme Programming) and, especially, pair-programming. No matter what flavor of pair-programming that you prefer, it involves two engineers sitting down at the same screen and solving the same problem together. One of the biggest benefits that you get is a fresh set of eyes on a problem, and of course, you now have two engineers who have "touched" the codebase instead of one. Sometimes you can have one engineer write the code, and the other write the tests and the comments. No matter how you slice it, it's all good stuff.

Chapter Overview

This chapter will walk you through obtaining and testing out your API key, get you comfortable making calls to the OpenAI JavaScript API for ChatGPT, and introduce you to how to get things done using other models as well. Furthermore, we'll be using ChatGPT as a pair-programmer to create an application that will allow us to input the name of a city and the time you'd like to arrive to work, then give you the weather and an estimated arrival time based on current traffic conditions! Sound exciting? Then let's jump right in.

© Bruce Hopkins Jr., Bruce Hopkins Sr. 2025
B. Hopkins Jr. and B. Hopkins Sr., *Creating ChatGPT Apps with JavaScript*,
https://doi.org/10.1007/979-8-8688-1221-7_2

You Have Node.js Already Installed, Right?

For obvious reasons, you can't do much in this book without having Node. js installed on your computer. Therefore, in order to check the version of Node that you have, just open a terminal window and execute:

```
node - v
```

If the output of the command shows you a version number, then you're all set!

Now, after executing the command above, if you see an error message, then you need to install Node.js for your specific operating system. If that's the case, then use ChatGPT or Google in order to get the instructions depending on your OS, and then open a new terminal window and execute the command above in order to see the version that you have.

Installing (or Updating) the OpenAI Node.js Library with npm

In order to use the OpenAI library with JavaScript, the minimum supported version of Node compatible is version 18, although the code examples were tested with version 20. Now that you have all the prerequisites, it's time to install the OpenAI Node.js library itself. Go back to your terminal window, and execute the following command:

```
npm install openai
```

The command above will install the OpenAI library for you if it doesn't already exist and will update the library to the most recent version it's already there.

Three Ways to Set Your API Key

When setting up your API key for the OpenAI API, there are different methods to choose from, each designed for specific project needs and security concerns.

Option #1: Setting a System-Wide Environment Variable

The environment variable approach establishes a system-wide environment variable for API key storage. This provides a centralized point for key management, simplifying deployment across diverse projects.

Let's look at the steps on how we'd go about doing it.

For Mac OS

First off, open Terminal. You can find it in the applications folder or use spotlight (Command + Space) to search for it.

Next, edit your bash profile. For older MacOS versions, you'd use the command nano ~/.bash_profile. Users of newer MacOS versions will need to use nano ~/.zshrc. This will open the profile file in a text editor.

Now let's add your environment variable. In the editor, add the line below, replacing "your-api-key-here" with your actual API key without the single quotation marks.

```
export OPENAI_API_KEY='your-api-key-here'
```

Let's save and exit by pressing Ctrl+O to write the changes, then pressing Ctrl+X to close the editor.

Now you're going to load your profile by using source ~/.bash_profile for older Mac OS versions and source ~/.zshrc for the newer Mac OS versions. This will load the updated profile.

Finally, we're going to verify that we've done everything correctly. In the terminal, type echo $OPENAI_API_KEY. If everything went well, you should see the value of your API key.

```
echo $OPENAI_API_KEY
```

For Windows

Start by opening the command prompt. You can find it by searching "cmd" in the Start/Windows menu.

Now we're going to set the environment variable in the current session by using the command below, replacing "your-api-key-here" with your actual API key. This command sets the OPENAI_API_KEY for the current session.

```
setx OPENAI_API_KEY 'your-api-key-here'
```

You can make the setup permanent by adding the variable through system properties:

- Right-click "This PC" or "My Computer" and select "Properties."

- Click "Advanced system settings."

- Click the "Environment Variables" button.

- In the "System variables" section, click "New..." and enter OPENAI_API_KEY as the variable name and your API key as the variable value.

To make sure everything is working properly, reopen the command prompt and type the command below to verify the setup. It should display your API key.

```
echo %OPENAI_API_KEY%
```

For Linux

To set the environment variable for the current session, open a terminal window and use the export command. Replace "your-api-key-here" with your actual API key.

Listing 2-1. Adding an Environment Variable on Your Hard Drive on Linux

```
export OPENAI_API_KEY='your-api-key-here'
```

To make the environment variable persistent across sessions, you can add it to your shell's configuration file, such as ~/.bashrc for Bash. Here's how you can do it:

Open the configuration file in a text editor. For example:

```
nano ~/.bashrc
```

Add the following line at the end of the file:

```
export OPENAI_API_KEY='your-api-key-here'
```

Save the file and exit the text editor.

To apply the changes immediately, you can either close and reopen the terminal or run:

```
source ~/.bashrc
```

To verify that the environment variable is set correctly, you can echo its value in the terminal. This command should display your API key:

```
echo $OPENAI_API_KEY
```

Option #2: Creating a .env File

Using a system-wide environment variable is great for making the API key accessible by any application or script running on the machine. However, if your use case is a little more simplistic, we can simply create a local variable accessible within just the scope of a particular program or script. It's also useful for situations in which different projects necessitate different keys, so you can prevent conflicts in key usage. Let's dive right in!

We're going to start by creating a local .env file. This file will hold your API key, ensuring it's only utilized by the designated project. Navigate to the project folder where you intend to create the .env file.

Note   To prevent your .env file from being unintentionally shared via version control, create a .gitignore file in your project's root directory. Add a line with .env to ensure the confidentiality of your API key and other sensitive information.

Next, use the terminal or an IDE to create both the .gitignore and .env files. Copy your API key and replace "your-api-key-here" with your actual API key without the single quotation marks.

At this point, your .env file should look like this:

```
OPENAI_API_KEY='your-api-key-here'
```

Finally, you can import the API key into your Node.js code using the following snippet:

Listing 2-2. Importing Your .env File Into Your Node.js Application

```
import OpenAI from "openai";
import "dotenv/config";

// Create a new open ai client
```

```
const openai = new OpenAI({
  apiKey: process.env["OPENAI_API_KEY"],
});
```

Of course, you'll need to install the dotenv package if you don't have it already. Just execute:

```
npm install dotenv
```

Option #3: Hard Coding the API Key Directly in Your Application (Take with Caution)

This last method isn't recommended for long-term use because of security reasons. But, for the sake of knowing how things work, we're going to cover how you can hard code your API key into your application if you want to quickly test out your API key to make sure it's working.

To begin, you'll assign the API key to a variable within the JavaScript code. Replace "YOUR_API_KEY" with the actual API key you received from OpenAI. Ensure that this API key is kept secure and not shared publicly.

Next, you'll initialize the OpenAI client within your Node.js script. This is done by instantiating the OpenAI class with the api_key parameter set to the API key. By providing the API key during initialization, you enable the OpenAI client to access the services offered by the OpenAI API. This step ensures that your Node.js script can communicate with the OpenAI API using the specified API key.

Listing 2-3. Coding Your API Key Directly into Your Application

```
import OpenAI from "openai";
import "dotenv/config";

const API_KEY = "YOUR_API_KEY";
```

```
const openai = new OpenAI({
  apiKey: API_KEY,
});
```

Now let's make our first application with the OpenAI API and test out the key at the same time by getting a list of models available within the OpenAI API.

Note   From this point on, the code examples will be accessing our API key with a local .env file.

Creating Your First JavaScript ChatGPT App: list-models

We're actually going to accomplish two tasks at once here. We're going to create a basic Node.js script using the OpenAI APIs, and in the process, we're going to verify that we've properly obtained an API key. So, needless to say, in case you haven't done so already, follow the instructions in Chapter 1 to create your OpenAI developer account and obtain your API key. Going forward, all the code samples in this book require a valid API key.

Using openai.models.list( ) to Get a List of Available Models

One of the most basic (but also essential) capabilities that we can get a list of available models. Why, you may ask? The ChatGPT website only exposes a handful of models available, and the Playground adds a few more that you can use. However, by invoking openai.models.list(), you get a list that specifies the name of every model, and there's a lot to choose from!

Handling the Response

> **Note**   Since objects can contain Arrays (which can be hard to represent in a table), we're using the following notation "↳" to indicate the elements of the Array. As you can see from Table 2-1, "id," "object," "created," and "owned_by" are all elements of the "data" Array in the response.

Table 2-1. *The Structure of the Model Object*

Field	Type	Description
object	String	This always returns the literal, "list"
data	Array	An Array of AI models offered by OpenAI
↳ id	String	The unique ID of the AI model, which is essentially the full name of the model
↳ object	String	This always returns the literal, "model"
↳ created	integer	The creation date for the model
↳ owned_by	String	The name of the organization that owns the model

Now that we have the details of the Model object, let's talk about how we can test our API key we obtained in the first chapter. There are actually a few ways to do this.

Using Your API Key to Get a List of Available Models with the OpenAI API

With our API key set up in a local .env file, we're going to use the following code to get a list of models available within the OpenAI API, which will then be printed into our terminal.

Listing 2-4. Getting a List of Models Available with the OpenAI API by Calling the models.list() Function

```
import OpenAI from "openai";
import "dotenv/config";

// Create openai client
const openai = new OpenAI({
  apiKey: process.env["OPENAI_API_KEY"],
});

async function main() {
  // Get the model list from the openai client
  const model_list = await openai.models.list();

  // Save the model names to a variable
  const model_names_list = model_list.data.map((model) =>
  model.id);

  // Loop through the names and log them.
  for (const name of model_names_list) {
    console.log(name);
  }
}

main();
```

After running the code in Listing 2-4, Listing 2-5 shows all the models that are available for us to use:

Listing 2-5. The List of Available Models

```
o1
o1-mini
dall-e-3
gpt-4o-mini
text-embedding-3-large
text-embedding-3-small
gpt-4-0125-preview
text-embedding-ada-002
dall-e-2
tts-1
tts-1-hd-1106
tts-1-1106
tts-1-hd
gpt-4
babbage-002
gpt-4-turbo-preview
gpt-4o-2024-08-06
gpt-3.5-turbo
gpt-4o
gpt-3.5-turbo-1106
whisper-1
gpt-3.5-turbo-16k
gpt-3.5-turbo-instruct-0914
gpt-3.5-turbo-0125
gpt-4-0613
gpt-3.5-turbo-instruct
gpt-4-1106-preview
```

```
chatgpt-4o-latest
gpt-4-turbo-2024-04-09
davinci-002
gpt-4-turbo
gpt-4o-2024-05-13
gpt-4o-mini-2024-07-18
```

As you can see in the list above, as a developer, we have more AI models available to us that are not even exposed to anyone who's using the Chat Playground!

So now, we're at the point where we can programmatically invoke the Open AI APIs using our API key. In the rest of this chapter, we're going to see what it's like to use ChatGPT as a pair-programmer in order to allow us to quickly build JavaScript applications.

However, we first need to put some thought into the prompts that we need to give to ChatGPT.

Wait, How Many Tokens Are in My Prompt?

At a certain point, you're going to start thinking about the prompts that you plan to send to ChatGPT and give considerable thought to the token limitations (and the costs) regarding the model that you want to use. In case you forgot, be sure to refer back to Table 1-1 for a list of models and the price of the tokens. Additionally, OpenAI created a simple-to-use website that allows you to see how many tokens are in your prompt, as shown in Figure 2-1.

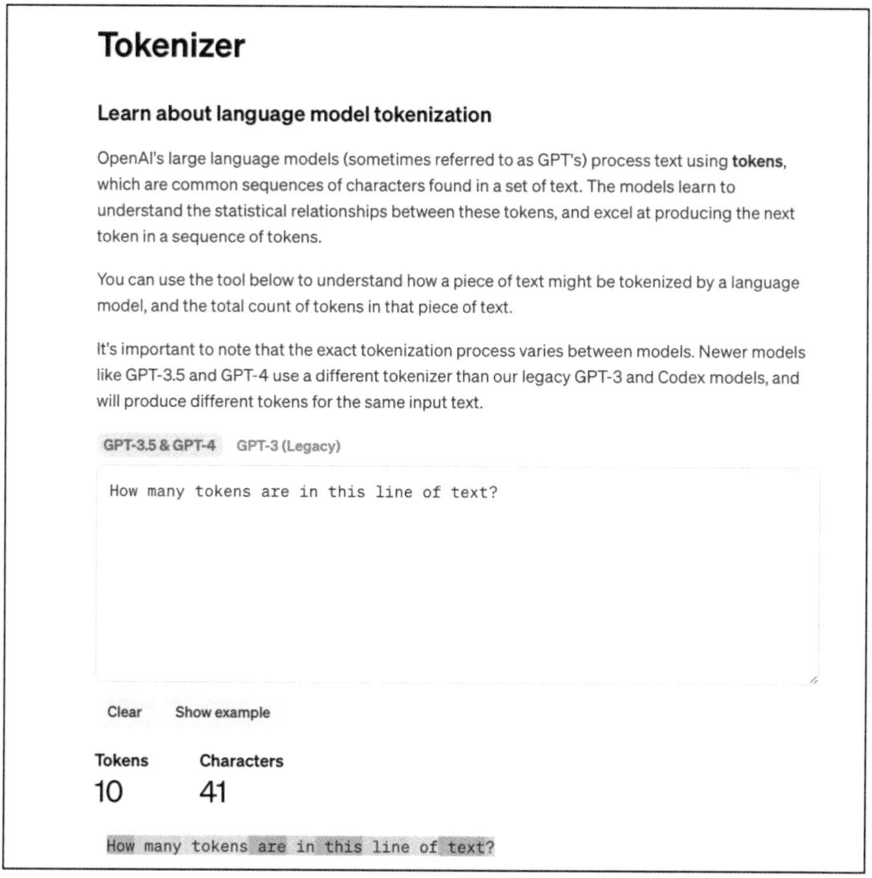

Tokenizer

Learn about language model tokenization

OpenAI's large language models (sometimes referred to as GPT's) process text using **tokens**, which are common sequences of characters found in a set of text. The models learn to understand the statistical relationships between these tokens, and excel at producing the next token in a sequence of tokens.

You can use the tool below to understand how a piece of text might be tokenized by a language model, and the total count of tokens in that piece of text.

It's important to note that the exact tokenization process varies between models. Newer models like GPT-3.5 and GPT-4 use a different tokenizer than our legacy GPT-3 and Codex models, and will produce different tokens for the same input text.

GPT-3.5 & GPT-4   GPT-3 (Legacy)

```
How many tokens are in this line of text?
```

Clear   Show example

Tokens   Characters
10   41

How many tokens are in this line of text?

Figure 2-1. *The ChatGPT Tokenizer Can Give You a Quick Count of the Tokens in Your Prompt*

ChatGPT Token Counter
https://platform.openai.com/tokenizer

Using ChatGPT As a Pair-Programmer to Build a Weather Application

Now that we've made sure that our API key works, it's time to start writing our first project with ChatGPT. This is the exciting part! We're going to use ChatGPT to help us create an application in JavaScript that will give us the weather and the time it'll take us to get to work from the location of our home to work. Sounds impressive, doesn't it?

Setting Up the Prompt

Let's ask ChatGPT how we should get started. Now is a good time to practice Prompt Engineering. We're going to explain to ChatGPT what we want and see what it comes up with. Listing 2-6 shows the prompt we used.

Listing 2-6. PROMPT. Asking ChatGPT to Help Us Make a Weather App for Productivity

```
I need a simple node.js application that will allow me to type
my city into the console and use Accuweather API to give me the
weather for the city
```

This is the code we got in the response (Listing 2-7):

Listing 2-7. Response. The Code and Instructions How to Create a Basic Weather App

```
Certainly! Below is a step-by-step guide to creating a simple
Node.js application that fetches weather data from the
```

AccuWeather API for a given city.

Step 1: Set Up Your Node.js Project

1. **Initialize a new Node.js project:**

    ```bash
    mkdir weather-app
    cd weather-app
    npm init -y
    ```

2. **Install necessary packages:**
    ```bash
    npm install axios readline-sync dotenv
    ```

Step 2: Set Up AccuWeather API

1. **Sign up for an AccuWeather API key:**
   Go to [AccuWeather Developer Portal](https://developer.
   accuweather.com/) and sign up for an API key.

2. **Create a `.env` file in your project root to store your
API key:**
    ```plaintext
    ACCUWEATHER_API_KEY=your_api_key_here
    ```

Step 3: Write the Application Code

Create a file named `index.js` in the project root and add the
following code:

```javascript
const axios = require("axios");
```

```javascript
const readlineSync = require("readline-sync");
require("dotenv").config();

const apiKey = process.env.ACCUWEATHER_API_KEY;
const baseUrl = "http://dataservice.accuweather.com";

async function getCityKey(city) {
  const url = `${baseUrl}/locations/v1/cities/search`;
  try {
    const response = await axios.get(url, {
      params: {
        apikey: apiKey,
        q: city,
      },
    });
    if (response.data && response.data.length > 0) {
      return response.data[0].Key;
    } else {
      console.log("City not found.");
      process.exit(1);
    }
  } catch (error) {
    console.error("Error fetching city key:", error);
    process.exit(1);
  }
}

async function getWeather(cityKey) {
  const url = `${baseUrl}/currentconditions/v1/${cityKey}`;
  try {
    const response = await axios.get(url, {
      params: {
        apikey: apiKey,
      },
```

```
    });
    if (response.data && response.data.length > 0) {
      return response.data[0];
    } else {
      console.log("Weather data not found.");
      process.exit(1);
    }
  } catch (error) {
    console.error("Error fetching weather data:", error);
    process.exit(1);
  }
}

async function main() {
  const city = readlineSync.question("Enter your city: ");
  const cityKey = await getCityKey(city);
  const weather = await getWeather(cityKey);

  console.log(`Weather in ${city}:`);
  console.log(
    `Temperature: ${weather.Temperature.Metric.
    Value}°${weather.Temperature.Metric.Unit}`
  );
  console.log(`Weather Text: ${weather.WeatherText}`);
}

main();
```

Step 4: Run the Application

1. **Run your application:**

```bash
node index.js
```

2. **Enter your city when prompted:**
   ```plaintext
   Enter your city: [Your City Name]
   ```

You should see the current weather conditions for the city you entered.

Summary

This simple Node.js application uses the AccuWeather API to fetch and display the current weather for a specified city. It uses "axios" to make HTTP requests, "readline-sync" to get user input from the console, and "dotenv" to manage environment variables securely.

That's fantastic, and also quite thorough! So let's follow the steps provided in the response, and later we can continue the conversation to make some changes to the code.

Creating a Weather App with the AccuWeather API

As the instructions stated, we first need to set up an account with Accuweather. Go to https://developer.accuweather.com/ and click the **Register** link to sign up (Figure 2-2).

Figure 2-2. *Accuweather Homepage for Developers*

After signing in, navigate over to **My Apps** (Figure 2-3).

Figure 2-3. *Navigating to the My Apps Tab on the Accuweather Developer Portal*

Once you're on the **My Apps** tab, you're going to want to **Add a new App** in order to get an API key to use in our application (Figure 2-4).

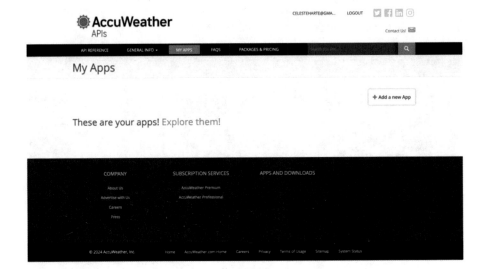

Figure 2-4. *Creating a New App with Accuweather*

As you set things up, you'll need to name your app and answer benign questions like where the API will be used and what you want to do with the API. As you can see in Figure 2-5, we've called our AccuWeather app "Weather Tracker."

Add App

App Name *

Weather Tracker

Internal name: weather-tracker Edit

Products*
Core Weather

⦿ Core Weather Limited Trial
○ None

MinuteCast

○ MinuteCast Limited Trial
○ None

Where will the API be used? *

Other

What will you be creating with this API? *

☐ Partner App
☐ Internal App
☑ Productivity App
☐ Weather App

What programming language is your APP written in? *

Python

Is this for Business to Business or Business to Consumer use? *

○ Business to Business
⦿ Business to Consumer

Is this Worldwide or Country specific use? *

⦿ Worldwide

Figure 2-5. *Adding Specifications for Our Accuweather App*

The most important configuration to enable here is where you're being asked to specify the product you're intending to use. **Be sure to enable the Core Weather Limited Trial**.

It may take some time for your application to be approved, but usually this is a very quick process. When it's done, you'll see your new application on the **My Apps** page, which will include your API key! Mission accomplished (Figure 2-6).

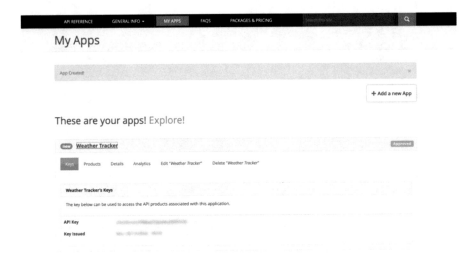

Figure 2-6. *Seeing Your Newly Created App on the Accuweather Developer Portal*

Refining Our Prompt with Prompt Engineering

Now, with everything all together, when you run the code, the application will ask you to input the name of a city.

```
Enter your city:
```

Once you provide a valid city name, you should find that everything runs smoothly, and you'll get a response that looks something like this (obviously, the forecast will change depending on what city you decide to enter and, well, what the weather is like the day you run it).

Listing 2-8. Using ChatGPT As Our Pair-Programmer, We Built a Fully Functioning Weather App in Only a Few Minutes

```
Weather in New York:
Temperature: 23.3°C
Weather Text: Cloudy
```

We get a nice, basic description of the weather in New York City from running the code, but there are a couple of things we can improve on.

AccuWeather has icons for various weather conditions. Right now, we can see that the weather in New York is currently cloudy, but we could also get a longer description that describes the weather for the rest of the day. Additionally, for those of us who live in the United States, it makes sense to see the temperature in Fahrenheit. So let's get ChatGPT to help us make those changes for us.

Since ChatGPT can retain the context, we're going to prompt ChatGPT in the same Chat conversation as in Listing 2-9:

Listing 2-9. Prompting ChatGPT to Change the Code to Get a More Detailed Response from the AccuWeather API

```
Thank you. I would like to make a few changes to this code.
•    Instead of using Celcius retrieve the temperature in
     Fahrenheit
•    Make an API call to get an icon number and an icon url to
     print in the response
•    Make an API call to get a weather description in the
     response
```

This is the answer we got from ChatGPT (Listing 2-10).

Listing 2-10. Response from ChatGPT to Modify the Code in Our Weather Application

```
Sure! Let's modify the code to include the following changes:
```

1. Retrieve the temperature in Fahrenheit instead of Celsius.
2. Get an icon number and an icon URL to print in the response.
3. Include a weather description in the response.

Updated Code

Here is the updated `index.js`:

```javascript
const axios = require("axios");
const readlineSync = require("readline-sync");
require("dotenv").config();

const apiKey = process.env.ACCUWEATHER_API_KEY;
const baseUrl = "http://dataservice.accuweather.com";
const iconBaseUrl = "https://developer.accuweather.com/sites/
default/files";

async function getCityKey(city) {
  const url = `${baseUrl}/locations/v1/cities/search`;
  try {
    const response = await axios.get(url, {
      params: {
        apikey: apiKey,
        q: city,
      },
    });
    if (response.data && response.data.length > 0) {
      return response.data[0].Key;
    } else {
      console.log("City not found.");
      process.exit(1);
    }
  } catch (error) {
```

```javascript
    console.error("Error fetching city key:", error);
    process.exit(1);
  }
}

async function getWeather(cityKey) {
  const url = `${baseUrl}/currentconditions/v1/${cityKey}`;
  try {
    const response = await axios.get(url, {
      params: {
        apikey: apiKey,
      },
    });
    if (response.data && response.data.length > 0) {
      return response.data[0];
    } else {
      console.log("Weather data not found.");
      process.exit(1);
    }
  } catch (error) {
    console.error("Error fetching weather data:", error);
    process.exit(1);
  }
}

function getIconUrl(iconNumber) {
  const iconNumberString = iconNumber.toString().
  padStart(2, "0");
  return `${iconBaseUrl}/${iconNumberString}-s.png`;
}

async function main() {
  const city = readlineSync.question("Enter your city: ");
```

```javascript
  const cityKey = await getCityKey(city);
  const weather = await getWeather(cityKey);

  const temperatureF = weather.Temperature.Imperial.Value;
  const weatherText = weather.WeatherText;
  const iconNumber = weather.WeatherIcon;
  const iconUrl = getIconUrl(iconNumber);

  console.log(`Weather in ${city}:`);
  console.log(`Temperature: ${temperatureF}°F`);
  console.log(`Weather Description: ${weatherText}`);
  console.log(`Icon URL: ${iconUrl}`);
}

main();
```

Explanation of Changes

1. **Fahrenheit Temperature**: The `Temperature.Imperial.Value` is used to get the temperature in Fahrenheit.
2. **Icon Number and URL**: A helper function `getIconUrl` is created to format the icon number and construct the URL for the icon image.
3. **Weather Description**: The `WeatherText` field is used to include a weather description.

Running the Application

After making these changes, run your application with the same command:

```bash
node index.js
```

Enter your city when prompted, and you will get the current weather conditions, temperature in Fahrenheit, weather description, and an icon URL.

This updated code ensures that you have all the required information displayed in the console, including the weather icon URL.

When we run this code, we get exactly what we were looking for. We'll enter a valid city name again (New York City, in our case), and this is the response we got (Listing 2-11):

Listing 2-11. Response from the AccuWeather API After Running the Modified Code

```
Enter your city: New York
Weather in New York:
Temperature: 63°F
Weather Description: Mostly cloudy
Icon URL: https://developer.accuweather.com/sites/default/
files/38-s.png
```

Now that our code works exactly the way we want it to, let's try another example.

Using ChatGPT As a Pair-Programmer to Build an Application That Estimates Distance and Arrival Time

The next thing we're going to want to do is start making an application that can give us an estimated arrival time and distance from one place to another, for example, from the house to the office. Let's use the Google Maps API to get this done.

Creating a Project with Google Maps Platform API

Most people already have a Gmail account, but on the off chance that you don't, be sure to create one before proceeding.

Google has a mountain of APIs for almost everything you can think of. However, since we're trying to accomplish tasks that require geolocation data, we're going to need to go directly to the APIs for Google Maps (as shown in Figure 2-7) which is located at `https://developers.google.com/maps/documentation`.

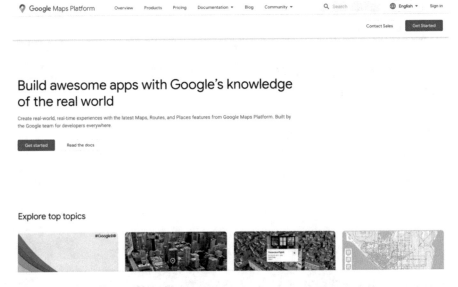

Figure 2-7. *The Google Maps Platform Homepage*

On the Google Maps Platform page, click **Getting Started** to set up your account for using the APIs. After following the steps Google presents you with, you'll be taken to the page shown in Figure 2-7, where you can see the different APIs available with the Google Maps Platform. But what'll probably catch your attention first is the fact that you still have to **Finish Account Setup**.

Finishing your account set up (see Figure 2-8) will compose of entering credit card information so you can start the free trial that will allow you $200 worth of credit, which is more than enough for the purposes of our testing.

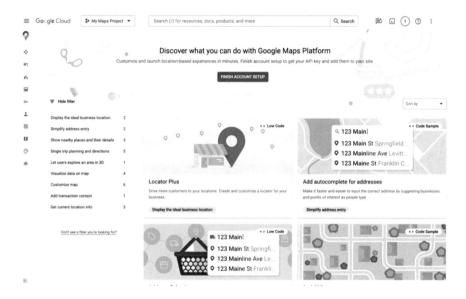

Figure 2-8. *Finishing Your Google Maps Platform Account SetUp*

After properly setting up your account, you'll be greeted by a welcome page. On the left, you'll find a menu icon you can click to reveal a list of services you have access to. You want to navigate to **Apps & Services**, and then click **Library** (as shown in Figures 2-9 and 2-10).

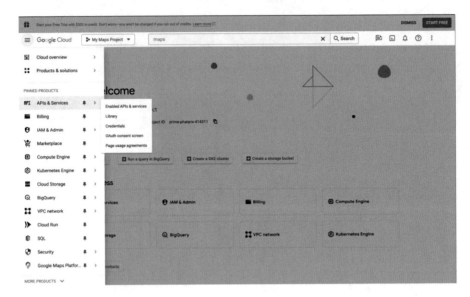

Figure 2-9. *Navigating to the APIs & Services Tab on the Google Maps Platform*

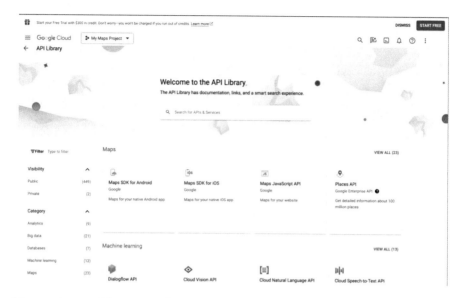

Figure 2-10. *The API Library Page*

You're going to want to click **Maps JavaScript API** and then **Enable** it, as shown in Figure 2-11.

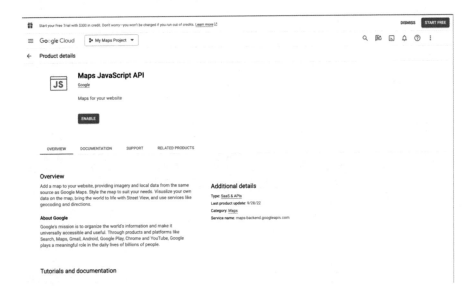

Figure 2-11. *Enabling the JavaScript API*

After enabling the JavaScript API, go back twice and open the menu again, and then click the **Google Maps Platform** to see the dashboard for Google Maps.

From here, we're going to be looking at another side menu that looks similar to the one from before, but here we're going to click **Apps & Services** again to see a different page this time. From here, you can click **Routes** to enable it, as shown in Figure 2-12.

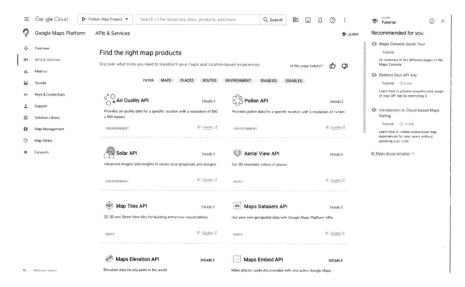

Figure 2-12. *Enabling the Routes API*

Once you've enabled the API we need, navigate to the **Keys & Credentials** tab and **Create a new API key** (Figure 2-13).

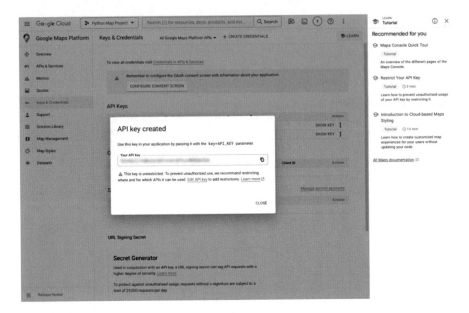

Figure 2-13. *The Keys and Credentials Page on the Google Maps Platform*

Now that we have our Google Maps API key, we can make use of ChatGPT to be our pair-programmer again. Our end goal is to have an app that tells us how far away is the destination and how long will it take to get there. By the way, here's a fun fact – the Google Maps Routes API factors in real-time traffic congestion data on the roads when you ask for the estimated travel time, so this makes our application perfect for productivity!

Now, in order to show the flexibility of ChatGPT as a pair-programmer, let's take two different approaches to achieve the same goal.

Approach #1: Using ChatGPT to Take a cURL Command and Convert It to JavaScript

In this first approach, instead of reading the Google Maps Platform documentation, we're actually going to cut to the chase and give ChatGPT the cURL command to invoke the API. you need and show you how to use ChatGPT to convert it to JavaScript for you. You're welcome.

Listing 2-12 is the cURL command from the Google Maps Platform documentation:

Listing 2-12. cURL Command for Using the Google Maps Routes API

```
curl -X POST -d '{
  "origin":{
    "location":{
      "latLng":{
        "latitude": 37.419734,
        "longitude": -122.0827784
      }
    }
  },
  "destination":{
    "location":{
      "latLng":{
        "latitude": 37.417670,
        "longitude": -122.079595
      }
    }
  },
  "travelMode": "DRIVE",
  "routingPreference": "TRAFFIC_AWARE",
```

```
  "departureTime": "2023-10-15T15:01:23.045123456Z",
  "computeAlternativeRoutes": false,
  "routeModifiers": {
    "avoidTolls": false,
    "avoidHighways": false,
    "avoidFerries": false
  },
  "languageCode": "en-US",
  "units": "IMPERIAL"
}' \
-H 'Content-Type: application/json' -H 'X-Goog-Api-Key: YOUR_
API_KEY' \
-H 'X-Goog-FieldMask: routes.duration,routes.
distanceMeters,routes.polyline.encodedPolyline' \
'https://routes.googleapis.com/directions/v2:computeRoutes'
```

Remember, the best practice is to separate the instructions from the content with three hashes (###) to get the best results. Listing 2-13 has the full prompt we gave to ChatGPT:

Listing 2-13. PROMPT. Asking ChatGPT to Convert cURL to JavaScript

```
I'm coding in JavaScript and trying to build an application
that makes a request to the Google Maps API and pull down the
amount of time it'll take to get from one location to the
other. This is the cURL code that would accomplish that goal.
Help me convert this to something I can use in JavaScript:
###
curl -X POST -d '{ "origin":{ "location":{ "latLng":{
"latitude": 37.419734, "longitude": -122.0827784 } } },
"destination":{ "location":{ "latLng":{ "latitude": 37.417670,
"longitude": -122.079595 } } }, "travelMode": "DRIVE",
```

```
"routingPreference": "TRAFFIC_AWARE", "departureTime":
"2023-10-15T15:01:23.045123456Z", "computeAlternativeRoutes":
false, "routeModifiers": { "avoidTolls": false,
"avoidHighways": false, "avoidFerries": false },
"languageCode": "en-US", "units": "IMPERIAL" }'
-H 'Content-Type: application/json' -H 'X-Goog-Api-Key: YOUR_
API_KEY'
-H 'X-Goog-FieldMask: routes.duration,routes.
distanceMeters,routes.polyline.encodedPolyline'
'https://routes.googleapis.com/directions/v2:computeRoutes
```

This is the code we got in the response from ChatGPT (Listing 2-14):

Listing 2-14. Response. Getting a Response Back from ChatGPT with Useable Javascript Code

To convert the provided cURL command to JavaScript, you can use the `fetch` API. Here is how you can do it:

```javascript
const apiKey = "YOUR_API_KEY"; // Replace with your
                               actual API key
const url = "https://routes.googleapis.com/directions/
v2:computeRoutes";

const requestBody = {
  origin: {
    location: {
      latLng: {
```

```javascript
        latitude: 37.419734,
        longitude: -122.0827784,
      },
    },
  },
  destination: {
    location: {
      latLng: {
        latitude: 37.41767,
        longitude: -122.079595,
      },
    },
  },
  travelMode: "DRIVE",
  routingPreference: "TRAFFIC_AWARE",
  departureTime: "2023-10-15T15:01:23.045123456Z",
  computeAlternativeRoutes: false,
  routeModifiers: {
    avoidTolls: false,
    avoidHighways: false,
    avoidFerries: false,
  },
  languageCode: "en-US",
  units: "IMPERIAL",
};

const requestOptions = {
  method: "POST",
  headers: {
    "Content-Type": "application/json",
    "X-Goog-Api-Key": apiKey,
    "X-Goog-FieldMask":
```

```
      "routes.duration,routes.distanceMeters,routes.polyline.
      encodedPolyline",
  },
  body: JSON.stringify(requestBody),
};

fetch(url, requestOptions)
  .then((response) => response.json())
  .then((data) => {
    // Process the data here
    console.log(data);
  })
  .catch((error) => {
    console.error("Error:", error);
  });
```

Explanation:

1. **API Key:** Ensure you replace `'YOUR_API_KEY'` with your
actual Google Maps API key.
2. **URL:** The URL for the Google Maps Directions API endpoint
remains the same.
3. **Request Body:** The request body is defined as a
JavaScript object and then converted to a JSON string using
`JSON.stringify()`.
4. **Request Options:**
   - `method: 'POST'` indicates that we are making a POST
   request.
   - `headers` includes the content type, API key, and the
   field mask.
   - `body` is the JSON string of the request body.

5. **fetch:** This makes the HTTP request and returns a
   promise.
   - `.then(response => response.json())` processes the
   response as JSON.
   - `.then(data => { ... })` processes the returned data.
   - `.catch(error => { ... })` handles any errors that occur
   during the fetch.

This code will send a POST request to the Google Maps API and
log the response data to the console. Adjust the processing
logic within the `.then(data => { ... })` block to fit the
needs of your application.

Note   In order for this code to run, you must set a date and time in
the "DEPARTURE-TIME" parameter that is beyond the time at which
you run the code. In other words, the departure time cannot be set in
the past. In this example, the date is set to a specific time in 2023,
because that was the timestamp in the original request. Therefore,
you need to adjust the code in the "DEPARTURE-TIME" parameter in
order for your code to run as expected.

After adjusting the timestamp and running the code, you should get a
response similar to Listing 2-15:

Listing 2-15. The Successful Response After Running the Code
from ChatGPT

```
{'routes': [{'distanceMeters': 773, 'duration': '158s',
'polyline': {'encodedPolyline': 'ipkcFjichVzQ@d@gU{E?'}}]}
```

Approach #2: Using ChatGPT to Avoid Reading a Lot of Documentation

As mentioned before, there is a *lot* of documentation to go through in the Google Maps Platform. If you take a cursory glance at the other capabilities available in the Routes API, you would see features to request various types of information such as air quality, pollen count, aerial views (like you'd see when you use Google Maps), and many other features of Google Maps you may normally take for granted. Do you know what geocoding is? Well, you'd have to find out the hard way if you went through the documentation on your own.

Reading through documentation is annoying, especially when we only want a few features in any given API or service. In a perfect world, we wouldn't even *need* to know what geocoding is in order to get our code working in different scenarios other than what's provided in the example code from Google.

We may not live in a perfect world, but we *don't* have to know what geocoding is, at least not anymore. We can simply use ChatGPT to get through the documentation we don't want to read.

Listing 2-16 shows the prompt to ChatGPT so you don't have to read any of the Google Maps Route API to get working code:

Listing 2-16. PROMPT. Asking ChatGPT to Avoid Reading Documentation

```
I need to use the Google Maps Platform's Routes API to pull
down information pertaining to how much time it'll take to get
from one destination to the other, as well as how much distance
is between the two points. How can I make an HTTP request in
JavaScript to get the information I'm looking for?
```

Listing 2-17 shows the response from ChatGPT:

Listing 2-17. Getting a Response Back from ChatGPT to Avoid Reading Documentation

To use the Google Maps Platform's Routes API in Node.js to get the travel time and distance between two points, you'll need to make an HTTP request to the API endpoint. Below are the steps and an example code snippet to help you get started:

1. **Get an API Key**: Ensure you have an API key from the Google Cloud Console with access to the Google Maps Platform.

2. **Install Axios**: We'll use the `axios` library to make HTTP requests. If you haven't already installed it, you can do so by running:

```sh
npm install axios
```

3. **Make the HTTP Request**: Create a Node.js script to make the HTTP request to the Routes API endpoint.

Here's an example script to achieve this:

```javascript
const axios = require("axios");

// Replace with your API key
const apiKey = "YOUR_GOOGLE_MAPS_API_KEY";
```

```javascript
// Function to get travel time and distance between two points
async function getTravelInfo(origin, destination) {
  const url = `https://maps.googleapis.com/maps/api/directions/
  json?origin=${encodeURIComponent(
    origin
  )}&destination=${encodeURIComponent(destination)}
  &key=${apiKey}`;

  try {
    const response = await axios.get(url);
    const data = response.data;

    if (data.status === "OK") {
      const route = data.routes[0];
      const leg = route.legs[0];
      const travelTime = leg.duration.text;
      const distance = leg.distance.text;

      console.log(`Travel time: ${travelTime}`);
      console.log(`Distance: ${distance}`);
    } else {
      console.error(`Error: ${data.status}`);
    }
  } catch (error) {
    console.error("Error making request", error);
  }
}

// Replace with your origin and destination
const origin = "New York, NY";
const destination = "Los Angeles, CA";

// Call the function
getTravelInfo(origin, destination);
```

Explanation

- **API Endpoint**: The URL for the Directions API endpoint is `https://maps.googleapis.com/maps/api/directions/json`.
- **Parameters**:
    - `origin`: The starting point for the route.
    - `destination`: The endpoint for the route.
    - `key`: Your API key.
- **Axios**: Used to make the HTTP GET request.
- **Response Handling**: The response contains a `status` field and a `routes` array. The first route's first leg contains the `duration` and `distance`.

Replace `'YOUR_GOOGLE_MAPS_API_KEY'` with your actual API key, and update the `origin` and `destination` with the desired locations.

Running the Script

1. Save the script to a file, e.g., `getTravelInfo.js`.
2. Run the script using Node.js:
   ```sh
   node getTravelInfo.js
   ```

This will print the travel time and distance between the specified origin and destination to the console.

If you run this code, you should get this very clean, very simple response:

```
Distance: 2,789 mi, Duration: 1 day 17 hours
```

Conclusion

Let's debunk a common myth and set the record straight: ChatGPT isn't some mind-reading wizard! As an AI tool, it can't replace the expertise of developers and architects. It can, however, complement the programming skills of developers and save you some time and effort when coding.

As you can see, one of the biggest benefits of using ChatGPT as a pair-programmer is that it can translate your natural language requests into runnable code. However, let's not forget the crucial role of human judgment whenever AI (not just ChatGPT) is put into practice. Ultimately, it's up to humans to decide whether to use, tweak, or toss out the result altogether.

CHAPTER 3

Creating a Basic ChatGPT Client in JavaScript

The purpose of this chapter is plain and simple. We're going to build the most powerful ChatGPT client available using only a few lines of code in JavaScript. This client will do a lot more than what you're able to do using the ChatGPT website and will provide you more options than what is available using the Chat Playground that we saw in Chapter 1.

Creating Our ChatGPT Client Application in JavaScript

Listing 3-1 is the code for our ChatGPT client in JavaScript. It's a simple client that allows us to use JSON to create `system` and `user` messages. We can also specify the desired model and configuration parameters such as the number of tokens to use.

© Bruce Hopkins Jr., Bruce Hopkins Sr. 2025
B. Hopkins Jr. and B. Hopkins Sr., *Creating ChatGPT Apps with JavaScript*,
https://doi.org/10.1007/979-8-8688-1221-7_3

Listing 3-1. The Javascript ChatGPT Client

```javascript
import OpenAI from "openai";
import "dotenv/config";

// Create a new open ai client
const openai = new OpenAI({
  apiKey: process.env["OPENAI_API_KEY"],
});

async function main() {
  const chatCompletion = await openai.chat.completions.create({
    messages: [
      {
        role: "system",
        content: "You are a JavaScript developer",
      },
      {
        role: "user",
        content: "Why is JavaScript use for web development?",
      },
    ],
    model: "gpt-4o",
    temperature: 0.85,
    top_p: 1,
    max_tokens: 1921,
    frequency_penalty: 0,
    presence_penalty: 0,
  });
  const result = chatCompletion.choices[0].message.content;
  console.log(result);
}

main();
```

As you analyze the code in Listing 3-1, you're going to see several things that are quite familiar from the Chat Playground such as the `model`, `messages`, `temperature`, and `tokens`.

Resist the Urge to Put Your API Key in a Web Application!

As you can see from the code in Listing 3-1, it only takes a few lines of code to make a fully functional ChatGPT client app in JavaScript. Later on in this chapter, we'll invoke the script and see the results.

Of course, we're all aware that one of the major benefits of JavaScript is that it can run both on the server side and within the browser on the client side. So, does this mean that it's a good idea to use this code in your React, Angular, or Vue projects to create an amazing experience for the visitors of your website?

Oh my dear sweet summer child. No, no, no, absolutely not. Remember that any and all code within your web applications is 100% visible to the world. In order for this code to work in the web browser, you need to provide your OpenAI API key to the code that will run in the web browser. Any competent developer can use a plethora of tools available to view the source code of your web application and discover your OpenAI API key. This means that they can easily rack up a massive bill for you and potentially use your API key in ways that will violate the terms of service of OpenAI.

Therefore, the best practice to make AI-enabled web applications is to make all your calls to the OpenAI APIs using Node.js on your server side. This way, there's no possibility of your API key to be exposed.

Using OpenAI.chat.completions. create() to Send Messages to ChatGPT

The OpenAI.chat.completions.create() method is a method that's basically a 1-to-1 representation of what you can do in the Chat Playground; therefore, this method should feel like second nature to you.

Table 3-1 describes the format of the parameters necessary to call the OpenAI.chat.completions.create() method. Although the table is lengthy, after a quick glance, you should see that only a few fields are actually required in order to successfully invoke the method.

The response to the method is called a ChatCompletion.

Examining the Method Parameters

Table 3-1. *The Structure of the Create ChatCompletion Object*

Field	Type	Required?	Description
model	String	Required	The ID of the model you want to use for the ChatCompletion.
			Compatible models include
			• gpt-4
			• gpt-4-0613
			• gpt-4-32k
			• gpt-4o
			• gpt-4o-mini
			• o1
			• o1-mini

(continued)

Table 3-1. (*continued*)

Field	Type	Required?	Description
messages	Array	Required	There are four types of messages, each with their own requirements:
			• System Message (see Table 3-2)
			• User Message (see Table 3-3)
			• Assistant Message (see Table 3-4)
			• Tool Message (see Table 3-5)
frequency_ penalty	Number or null default: 0	Optional	A number between -2.0 and 2.0.
			Positive values penalize tokens based on their existing frequency in the conversation history, reducing the likelihood of repeating the same lines verbatim
logit_bias	JSON Map default: null	Optional	Allows you to modify the likelihood of specific tokens appearing in the completion.
			You provide a JSON object that maps tokens (specified by their token ID in the tokenizer) to associated bias values from -100 to 100.
			This bias is added to the model's logits before sampling

(*continued*)

Table 3-1. (*continued*)

Field	Type	Required?	Description
logprobs	boolean or null	Optional, defaults to false	This parameter enables you to decide if the log probabilities of the output tokens should be returned.
			When set to true, it provides the log probabilities for each output token included in the message content.
			However, this feature is presently not supported by the gpt-4-vision-preview model.
max_tokens	integer or null	Optional	This parameter sets the maximum number of tokens that the generated Chat Completion can have.
n	integer or null default: 1	Optional	Specifies how many ChatCompletion choices the model should generate for each input message
presence_ penalty	Number or null default: 0	Optional	A number between -2.0 and 2.0.
			Positive values penalize new tokens based on whether they appear in the conversation history, encouraging the model to talk about new topics

(*continued*)

Table 3-1. (*continued*)

Field	Type	Required?	Description
response_ format	JSON object	Optional	You have two options:
			{ "type": "json_object" } for a JSON object response
			or
			{ "type": "text" } for a text response
			Note:
			It's crucial to remember that while operating in JSON mode, you need to explicitly command the model to generate JSON, either through a system or user directive.
			Failing to do so can cause the model to endlessly output whitespace until it hits the token cap, leading to a request that appears to be frozen.
			Additionally, be aware that if the finish_reason is "length", it suggests the generation went beyond the max tokens or the conversation exceeded the maximum allowable context length, which might result in the message being truncated.

(*continued*)

Table 3-1. (*continued*)

Field	Type	Required?	Description
seed	integer or null	Optional	By specifying a seed, the system will make an attempt to generate repeatable results. In theory, this means that if you make repeated requests with the same seed and parameters, you should expect to receive the same result.
			In order to get the seed value to put in the subsequent request, copy the system_ fingerprint from your last response
stop	String / list / null default: null	Optional	You can provide up to four sequences where the API should stop generating further tokens.
			This can be useful for controlling the length or content of responses.
stream	Boolean or null default: false	Optional	If "stream" is set to "true," partial message updates will be sent as server-sent events.
			This means tokens will be sent as data-only events as they become available, and the stream will end with a "data: [DONE]" message
temperature	Number or null default: 1	Optional	Valid values range between 0 and 2.
			Controls the randomness of the model's output.
			The best practice is to adjust the top_p or temperature, but not both.

(*continued*)

Table 3-1. (*continued*)

Field	Type	Required?	Description
tool_choice	String or JSON object	Optional	This parameter controls which (if any) function is called by the model. You have two options: "none" or "auto"
			Use "none" if you don't want the model to call a function.
			Use "auto" if you want the model to pick between generating a message or calling a function.
			Specifying a particular function via {"type": "function", "function": {"name": "my_function"}} forces the model to call that function.
			Please note that "none" is the default when no functions are present, and "auto" is the default if functions are present.
tools	Array	Optional	Optionally, you can specify a list of tools the model may call.
			Currently, only functions are supported as a tool.
			Use this to provide a list of functions the model may generate JSON inputs for.

(*continued*)

Table 3-1. (*continued*)

Field	Type	Required?	Description
top_logprobs	integer or null	Optional	This can be any integer from 0 to 5.
			It's used to determine the count of the most probable tokens to return at each token position, accompanied by their respective log probabilities.
			For this parameter to be applicable, logprobs must be enabled by setting it to true.
top_p	Number or null default: 1	Optional	Valid values range between 0 and 1.
			Indicates whether to consider few possibilities (0) or all possibilities (1).
			The best practice is to adjust the top_p or temperature, but not both.
user	String	Optional	This is a unique ID that you can optionally generate to represent your end user.
			This will help OpenAI monitor and detect abuse

OK, Table 3-1 appears to be a little daunting! However as mentioned earlier, only the model and messages are required parameters.

Additionally, we also have the code in Listing 3-1 above in order to show how the parameters are actually used within a real application.

So, as you can see, as a JavaScript developer, we have several options and parameters available to use that ordinary people can't do using the ChatGPT website or using the Chat Playground.

Now, the one parameter that needs the most detailed explanation is the messages parameter so let's analyze that further.

There Are Four Types of Messages

When invoking the ChatGPT API programmatically, there are four types of messages that you can provide to the API:

- System message
- User message
- Assistant message
- Tool message

The good news is that if you refer back to Chapter 1 where we explained how to use the Chat Playground, you can see that we've already have encountered the first three message types! The only new message type that we're not currently familiar with is the "tool message."

System Message (Array)

Table 3-2. *The Structure of the System Message*

Field	Type	Required?	Description
role	String	Required	This must be set to the String, "system"
content	String	Required	These are the instructions that you want the system to perform in the conversation
name	String	Optional	This is an optional name that you can provide the system

Listing 3-2 is a snippet from Listing 3-1 that shows how the system message is formatted:

Listing 3-2. Formatting the System Message

```
messages=[
    {
        "role": "system",
        "content": "You are a JavaScript developer"
    },
    ...
```

User Message (Array)

Table 3-3. *The Structure of the User Message*

Field	Type	Required?	Description
role	String	Required	This must be set to the String, "user"
content	String	Required	This String contains the actual message or question that you want to send to ChatGPT
name	String	Optional	This is an optional name that you can provide for yourself in the conversation

Listing 3-3 is a snippet from Listing 3-1 that shows how the user message is formatted:

Listing 3-3. Formatting the User Message

```
messages=[
    ...
    {
        "role": "user",
```

```
        "content": "Why is JavaScript typically used for
        data science?"
    }
...
```

Assistant Message (Array)

Note   In case you forgot, the Assistant Message is used to "remind" ChatGPT what it told you in a previous response. Ideally, this can allow you to continue a conversation that you had with it weeks or months in the past.

Table 3-4. *The Structure of the Assistant Message*

Field	Type	Required?	Description
role	String	Required	This must be set to the String, "assistant"
content	String	Required	This String contains the response from ChatGPT from a previous conversation
name	String	Optional	This is an optional name that you can provide for ChatGPT in the conversation
tool_calls	Array	Optional	If ChatGPT used a tool in a previous response, then include the tool that it specified here
↳ id	String	Required	This is the ID of the tool called by ChatGPT
↳ type	String	Required	This is the type of the tool called by ChatGPT. Only the literal, "function," is a valid tool
↳ function	Object	Required	This is the function that the model called

Listing 3-4 is a snippet from Listing 3-1 that shows how the user message is formatted:

Listing 3-4. Formatting the ASSISTANT Message

```
messages=[
...
    {
        "role": "assistant",
        "content": "JavaScript is typically used for data
        science for several reasons...”
    }
...
```

Tool Message (Array)

A Tool Message is an advanced type of message for a very specific use case. You can't use them on the ChatGPT website nor in the Chat Playground. Using a Tool Message and the tool parameter from Table 3-1, you can enable ChatGPT to "call a function" for you.

At first glance, you may be thinking, "Wow! ChatGPT will load my code and execute it for me in the Cloud? That's awesome!" Unfortunately, that's not the case.

By providing a function name and the parameters necessary to invoke it, ChatGPT will let you know whether to invoke the function and the parameters to put in the function. You will then need to call the function YOURSELF within your JavaScript code.

Table 3-5. *The Structure of the Tool Message*

Field	Type	Required?	Description
role	String	Required	This must be set to the String, "tool"
content	String	Required	This String contains the content of the tool message
tool_call_id	Array	Optional	This is the id of the tool call

Note   Due to the fact that Tool messages and function calling are advanced topics, we're not going to explain them further in this book. However, it's good to be aware of all the four types of messages that exist. This book will focus on System, User, and Assistant messages.

Running Our Basic ChatGPT Client

So, after running the code we created in Listing 3-1, we can expect a response that will look something like this in Listing 3-5.

Listing 3-5. ChatGPT Explains Why JavaScript Is So Awesome

JavaScript is used for web development for several reasons:

1. Interactivity: JavaScript allows developers to create interactive elements on a website, such as forms, animations, and other interactive content. This enhances user experience and makes a website more dynamic.

2. Client-side processing: JavaScript is a client-side language, which means it runs on the user's web browser instead of the server. This results in faster load times and less strain on the server, especially for complex tasks.

3. Browser compatibility: JavaScript is supported by all modern web browsers without the need for plugins, making it accessible for almost all internet users.

4. Versatility: JavaScript can be used for both front-end and back-end development. This versatility makes it a valuable skill for full-stack developers.

5. Frameworks and Libraries: JavaScript has numerous libraries (like jQuery, React) and frameworks (like Angular, Vue) which facilitate easier and faster development.

6. JSON: JavaScript Object Notation (JSON) is a light-weight data interchange format that is easy for humans to read and write. It is easy for machines to parse and generate. This makes JavaScript particularly useful for APIs and configurations.

7. Community and resources: JavaScript has a large and active developer community, which means there are plenty of resources, tutorials, and third-party plugins available. This can make problem-solving and learning easier.

8. Real-time feedback: JavaScript allows for real-time feedback on websites. This is critical for tasks like form validation where you want to give feedback immediately, not after a page reload.

9. It's evolving: JavaScript is constantly evolving and new features are added regularly, making it an exciting language to work with.

So, as we take a brief look at Listing 3-5, we see that the response (called a `ChatCompletion`) is the answer to our question that we posed to ChatGPT in Listing 3-1 at the very beginning of the chapter. However, there's a lot of metadata around our response, and let's analyze the `ChatCompletion` object in more detail.

Handling the Response (`ChatCompletion`)

Table 3-6. *The Structure of the ChatCompletion Object Response*

Field	Type	Description
id	String	A distinct identifier for the ChatCompletion
choices	Array	A list of ChatCompletion options. There can be multiple options in the response if "n" is greater than 1 in Table 3-1
↳ finish_reason	String	Every response will include a finish_reason. The possible values for finish_reason are:
		stop: The API returned complete message, or a message terminated by one of the stop sequences provided via the stop parameter
		length: The model output was incomplete due to the max_tokens parameter in the request or token limit of the model itself
		tool_call: The model called a tool, such as a function
		content_filter: The response was terminated due to a violation of the content filters
		null: The API response still in progress or incomplete

(continued)

Table 3-6. (*continued*)

Field	Type	Description
↳ index	Integer	The index of the choice in the list of choices
↳ message	Object	A ChatCompletionMessage generated by the model. This is explained in further detail in Table 3-6
↳ logprobs	Object or Null	Log probability information for the choice
model	String	The model used for the ChatCompletion
system_fingerprint	String	Use this parameter as the "seed" in a subsequent request if you want to reproducible results in from a previous conversation
object	String	This always returns the literal, "chat.completion"
usage	Object	Usage statistics for the completion request
↳ completion_tokens	Integer	Number of tokens in the generated completion
↳ prompt_tokens	Integer	Number of tokens in the prompt
↳ total_tokens	Integer	The total count of tokens utilized in the request, including both the prompt and the completion

The most important item in the ChatCompletion object is the ChatCompletionMessage which is explained in more detail in Table 3-7.

ChatCompletionMessage

Table 3-7. *The Structure of the ChatCompletionMessage*

Field	Type	Description
role	String	This will always be the literal, "assistant"
content	String or null	This is a String that contains the response from ChatGPT to our request
tool_calls	Array	If you indicated in Table 3-1 that you want ChatGPT to call a tool (which is currently a function), then this list will exist in the ChatCompletionMessage
↳ id	String	This is the ID of the tool called by ChatGPT
↳ type	String	This is the type of the tool called by ChatGPT. Only the literal, "function," is a valid tool
↳ function	Object	This is the function and the parameters that the model called

Conclusion

In this chapter, we took our experiences from Chapters 1 and 2 and created a fully functioning ChatGPT client in JavaScript. In the code for our ChatGPT client, we saw some terms that we were already introduced to from the Chat Playground such as the model, messages, temperature, and tokens.

We also saw that, as JavaScript developers, OpenAI gives us a **TON OF ADDITIONAL OPTIONS** to invoke ChatGPT that aren't available to average everyday users or even to technical people who use the Chat Playground. In this chapter we took the time to explain these options, with a focus on the messages that we can send.

Now that we have a working ChatGPT client in JavaScript, let's see how to leverage it for the rest of the examples in the book!

CHAPTER 4

Using AI in the Enterprise! Creating a Text Summarizer for Slack Messages

In today's corporate world, it's extremely common for companies to have an instance of Slack (or Microsoft Teams) to organize themselves and use it as a central place of communication to everyone in the company. Now, if you've ever used Slack before, I think you know how easily a channel can become flooded with a ton of messages because **SOME** important thing happened **SOMEWHERE** in the company or the world.

Of course, the more responsibility that you have within the company (i.e., manager, team leader, architect, etc.), the more channels you're expected to participate in. In my opinion, Slack is a double-edged sword. You need to use it to do your job, but as a developer, you definitely can't attend a daily standup meeting and say, "Yesterday, uh, I spent all day reading Slack. No roadblocks."

Additionally, if you work for a company with clients in various time zones (which is quite common nowadays), it's pretty daunting to open Slack in the morning and see a ton of messages that were posted while you were away from the keyboard.

© Bruce Hopkins Jr., Bruce Hopkins Sr. 2025
B. Hopkins Jr. and B. Hopkins Sr., *Creating ChatGPT Apps with JavaScript*,
https://doi.org/10.1007/979-8-8688-1221-7_4

So, in this chapter, we're going to apply AI in the enterprise to make Slack more useful. We'll leverage the code in the previous chapter and create a Slack bot in JavaScript that will summarize the important conversations in a Slack channel. We're going to be utilizing ChatGPT's capabilities for text summarization and focus a bit more on **Prompt Engineering**.

So, What Is Prompt Engineering?

Simply stated, Prompt Engineering is the process of carefully crafting and refining prompts and input parameters to instruct and guide the behavior of ChatGPT and other AI models. It's basically the industry-wide term for creating the right input in order to get the result that you're looking for.

ChatGPT Is Here to Take Away Everyone's Jobs (Not Really)

It is our humble opinion that every company in the world is sitting on a gold mine of untapped information. If you are using any system that keeps a log of exchanges between employees, a database of support requests from your customers, or any large repository of text (yes this includes your email, Microsoft Exchange, and corporate Gmail), then, you have a large repository of unstructured text that is waiting to be utilized.

Therefore, the best use of ChatGPT is not to eliminate anyone's jobs. It should be used in order to augment and extend what team members in your company are already doing. As we saw in Chapter 2, as a software developer, ChatGPT can work as a very effective Pair-Programmer. It is also very good at performing certain difficult tasks very efficiently and quickly. Therefore, the project of this chapter involves tackling a practical example of what can be done in order to make use of a large source of unstructured text.

92

You can use the ChatGPT client you created in Chapter 3 for the prompt engineering examples listed further on in this chapter, or you can use the playground mode feature we talked about in Chapter 1. Either way, let's dive right in.

Examining a Real-World Problem: Customer Support for a Software Company

Let's look at one of the most grueling tasks in software development: providing tech support. Imagine the joys of fielding calls and messages all day from people who might be frustrated, confused, or just in need of a solution while using your software. Here's some of the reasons why customer support is a tough nut to crack:

- Your end users and your customers are notoriously bad at explaining problems with your software.

- Level 1 technicians, often the first line of defense, typically handle the most basic issues or user errors. But when problems get more complex, users are escalated to Level 2.

- The mid-tier is a tricky place, because they have more knowledge and experience than the tech support staff at Level 1; however, they don't have the opportunity to directly get answers from the end user.

- Really bad problems get escalated to Level 3; however, these are the most expensive tech support staff because they have the most knowledge and experience. They have hands-on experience with the code as well as the servers and the infrastructure.

So let's work with a real-world example of a typical conversation within a typical tech support channel within Slack. Below is a list of the team members and their roles within a fictional company:

- Fatima (Customer Service Representative)

- John (Software Engineer)

- Dave (PM)

- Keith (CTO)

Listing 4-1 provides an example of a conversation between the team members at a software startup. Fatima, the customer service representative, lets the team know that their app is crashing immediately after launching (not a good problem to have). Keith, the CTO, steps in immediately to escalate the issue.

Listing 4-1. Team Members Within a Slack Channel Trying to Analyze a Customer's Problem

Fatima [16:00 | 02/08/2019]: Hey everyone, I have an urgent issue to discuss. I just got off a call with a client who's experiencing app crashes as soon as they load it. They're really frustrated. Can we get this sorted ASAP? ☹

Keith [16:01 | 02/08/2019]: Thanks for bringing this to our attention, Fatima. Let's jump on this right away. @John, can you take the lead in investigating the issue since our architect is out sick today?

John [16:02 | 02/08/2019]: Sure thing, Keith. I'll dive into the codebase and see if I can find any potential culprits for the crashes.

John [16:02 | 02/08/2019]: Fatima, could you gather some additional information from the client? Ask them about the specific device, operating system, and any recent updates they might have installed.

Fatima [16:03 | 02/08/2019]: Absolutely, John. I'll reach out to the client immediately and gather those details. Will update you all once I have them.

Dave [16:04 | 02/08/2019]: I understand the urgency here. Let's make sure we keep the client informed about our progress 💯 Fatima. We don't want them feeling left in the dark during this troubleshooting process.

Fatima [16:04 | 02/08/2019]: Definitely, Dave. 👍 I'll keep the client updated at regular intervals, providing them with any relevant information we uncover.

John [16:20 | 02/08/2019]: I've checked the codebase, and so far, I haven't found any obvious issues. It's strange that the app is crashing on load. Could it be a memory-related issue? Keith, do we have any recent reports of memory leaks or high memory usage?

Keith [16:22 | 02/08/2019]: I'll pull up the monitoring logs, John, and check if there have been any memory-related anomalies in recent releases. Let me get back to you on that.

Fatima [17:01 | 02/08/2019]: Quick update, everyone. The client is using an iPhone X running iOS 15.1. They mentioned that the issue started after updating their app a few days ago 🤤

Keith [17:05 | 02/08/2019]: Thanks for the update, Fatima. That's helpful information. John, let's focus on testing the latest app update on an iPhone X simulator with iOS 15.1 to see if we can replicate the issue.

John [17:06 | 02/08/2019]: Good idea, Keith. I'll set up the emulator and run some tests right away.

Keith [17:30 | 02/08/2019]: John, any progress on replicating the issue on the emulator?

John [17:32 | 02/08/2019]: Yes, Keith. I managed to reproduce the crash on the emulator. It seems to be related to a compatibility issue with iOS 15.1 😵. I suspect it's due to a deprecated method call. I'll fix it and run more tests to confirm.

John [18:03 | 02/08/2019]: Fixed the deprecated method issue, and the app is no longer crashing on load. It looks like we've identified and resolved the problem. I'll prepare a patch and send it to you, Keith, for review and deployment.

Keith [18:04 | 02/08/2019]: 🖐🖐🖐 Thank you, please provide me with the patch as soon as possible. Once I review it, we'll deploy the fix to the app store.

Dave [18:06 | 02/08/2019]: Great job, team! 🎉 John, please keep the client informed about the progress and let them know we have a fix ready for them on the next app update. Can someone make sure the release notes reflect this?

John [18:07 | 02/08/2019]: Will do, Dave. I'll update the client and ensure they're aware of the upcoming fix.

Keith [18:27 | 02/08/2019]: Patch reviewed and approved, John. Please proceed with updating the app in the store. Let's aim to have it done within the next hour.

John [18:26 | 02/08/2019]: Understood, Keith. I'm in the process of uploading it now.

Fatima [18:38 | 02/08/2019]: I just informed the client about the fix. They're relieved and grateful for our prompt response. Thanks, everyone, for your collaboration and quick action. It's a pleasure working with such a competent team!

Dave [18:40 | 02/08/2019]: Well done, team! Your efforts are greatly appreciated. We managed to turn this urgent problem around in record time. Let's keep up the good work! 👍

Prompt Engineering 101: Text Summarization

So, needless to say, no one wants to spend their day constantly scrolling through Slack channels reading about issues and problems that are on fire. We're going to utilize the capabilities of ChatGPT for text summarization. To keep things simple, let's try a few prompts to send the entire listing of the chat messages to ChatGPT in order for it to give us a usable summary of all the events that have happened.

Note   Please be aware the ChatGPT is nondeterministic. This simply means that even if you executed the same prompt with the same settings multiple times, you won't necessarily get a word-for-word response as shown in the listings in this chapter. However, they should be quite similar.

Prompt #1: "tl;dr"

This prompt is short, sweet, and to the point. In case you're not familiar
with it, it's a term used online frequently to briefly summarize a long
article. It literally stands for "Too Long; Didn't Read," which is how I feel
about a lot of conversations on Slack when I'm swamped with work.
Conveniently, ChatGPT can understand this simple term (I wouldn't
necessarily call it a word) as a prompt, and the results are pretty
impressive.

Listing 4-2. PROMPT. Asking for a Summarized Version of a Longer
Conversation

System: You are a helpful assistant
User: Fatima [16:00 | 02/08/2019]: Hey everyone, I have an
urgent ...
User: Tl;dr
Model: gpt-4o
Temperature: 1
Maximum length: 360
Top P: 1
Frequency penalty: 0
Presence penalty: 0

Notice how the number of tokens is kept small, at 360, which will
ultimately help ChatGPT to create a short response. Also see that the
temperature is left at 1 (the default value), but the Top P is increased all the
way to its maximum (which is 1). Therefore, it's important to play around
with temperature and other settings to control the tone and variety of
ChatGPT's responses.

Listing 4-3 shows ChatGPT's summarization of the conversation from
Listing 4-1.

Listing 4-3.   RESPONSE. Getting a Summarized Version of a Very
Long Conversation

```
The team quickly responds to a client's app crashing issue.
John investigates the codebase while Fatima gathers information
from the client. They discover a compatibility issue with iOS
15.1 and John fixes it. The patch is reviewed and approved,
and the app is updated in the store. The client is informed
and grateful for the quick resolution. The team is praised for
their collaboration and prompt action.
```

That's fantastic! It reduced that extremely long conversation down to
a simple and brief summary of only 68 words. As you can see, ChatGPT is
not replacing a job here; however, it will definitely make someone more
productive. Now, let's try a few more prompts, shall we?

Prompt #2: "Explain This in 3 Sentences or Less"

So, if "tl;dr" doesn't provide a brief enough explanation for you, then we
can tell ChatGPT to make things even simpler. ChatGPT does well with
parameters, so let's specify that the explanation shouldn't be any longer
than three sentences (Listing 4-4).

Listing 4-4.   PROMPT. Asking for a Shorter Version of a Longer
Conversation

```
System: You are a helpful assistant
User:   Fatima [16:00 | 02/08/2019]: Hey everyone, I have an
urgent ...
User: Explain this in 3 sentences or less.
```

Model: gpt-4o

Temperature: 1

Maximum length: 250

Top P: 0

Frequency penalty: 0

Presence penalty: 0

As you may have noticed, the temperature is set to 0.82 in this example. We really want ChatGPT to give us a concise answer here, so the "drier" the better.

Listing 4-5. RESPONSE. Getting a 3-Sentence Summary

A customer reported an urgent issue of app crashes to the team. John investigates the issue and asks Fatima to gather additional information from the client. They discover that the issue is related to a compatibility problem with iOS 15.1. John fixes the problem and Keith approves the deployment of the fix to the client's production environment.

Prompt #3: "I'm a Manager. Explain to Me What Happened"

When you don't want to sound like the one person that doesn't understand, ChatGPT has the capability to rephrase what has been said and break it down until it's very simple.

Listing 4-6. PROMPT. Asking for a Simplified Version of a More
Complex Conversation

System: You are a helpful assistant
User: Fatima [16:00 | 02/08/2019]: Hey everyone, I have an
urgent ...
User: Summarize this conversation and explain it to me like I'm
a manager with little technical experience.
Model: gpt-4o
Temperature: 0.82
Maximum length: 750
Top P: 1
Frequency penalty: 0
Presence penalty: 0

Again, the temperature is set below 1.0 so that ChatGPT can keep the
answer brief and easy to understand. We increased the token length so that
ChatGPT can take the time to explain some potentially technical concepts.

Listing 4-7. RESPONSE. Getting a Simplified Version of a More
Complex Conversation

In this conversation, Fatima brings up an urgent issue with a
client who is experiencing app crashes as soon as they load
it. Keith assigns John to investigate the issue since their
architect is out sick. John asks Fatima to gather additional
information from the client about their device, operating

system, and recent updates. Dave emphasizes the importance of keeping the client informed throughout the troubleshooting process.

John checks the codebase but doesn't find any obvious issues, so he suspects it could be a memory-related problem. Keith agrees to check for memory-related anomalies in recent releases. Fatima provides an update that the client is using an iPhone X running iOS 15.1 and mentioned that the issue started after updating the app. Keith suggests testing the latest app update on an iPhone X simulator with iOS 15.1 to replicate the issue.

John successfully reproduces the crash on the emulator and identifies a compatibility issue with iOS 15.1, possibly due to a deprecated method call. He fixes the issue and prepares a patch for review and deployment. Keith approves the patch and asks John to update the app in the store. Dave requests that the client be kept informed and that the release notes reflect the upcoming fix.

John uploads the patch and informs the client about the fix. Keith reviews and approves the patch, and John proceeds with updating the app in the store. Fatima informs the client about the fix, and they express relief and gratitude for the prompt response. Dave commends the team for their collaboration and quick action, emphasizing the importance of maintaining good work.

In summary, the team quickly addressed an urgent issue where a client's app was crashing on load. They investigated the issue, identified a compatibility problem with iOS 15.1, fixed

it, and prepared a patch for deployment. The client was kept
informed throughout the process, and the fix was successfully
implemented, resulting in a relieved and grateful client.

Prompt #4: "Give Me Suggestions on Next Steps"

In addition to making a summary that's easier to understand, ChatGPT can
explain in different styles and "tones." We're going to increase the top P to
0.75 because we want ChatGPT to think of more possibilities than what
is the default. We are also going to increase the presence penalty to 0.5
because we want to encourage a versatile response.

Listing 4-8. PROMPT. Asking to ChatGPT for Advice on the Best
Next Steps

System: You are a helpful assistant
User: Fatima [16:00 | 02/08/2019]: Hey everyone, I have an
urgent ...
User: I'm a QA engineer at the company. Give me suggestions on
next steps.
Model: gpt-4o
Temperature: 1
Maximum length: 1200
Top P: 0.75
Frequency penalty: 0
Presence penalty: 0.5

Listing 4-9. RESPONSE. Suggestions from ChatGPT on Possible Next Steps

As a QA engineer, here are some suggestions for next steps:

1. Test the patch: Once the patch has been deployed to the app store, thoroughly test it on various devices and operating systems to ensure that the issue has been resolved and there are no new bugs or regressions introduced.

2. Conduct regression testing: In addition to testing the specific issue, perform a comprehensive regression test to ensure that the fix does not have any unintended side effects on other functionalities of the app.

3. Communicate the fix to the client: Keep the client updated on the progress and let them know that the fix is available in the latest app update. Provide them with clear instructions on how to update their app and encourage them to test it on their end as well.

4. Monitor user feedback: Keep an eye on user feedback after the fix has been deployed. Encourage users to report any issues they encounter, and be proactive in addressing them promptly.

5. Document the issue and resolution: Create a detailed report documenting the issue, the steps taken to reproduce and resolve it, and any other relevant information. This will serve as a reference for future troubleshooting and help improve the development process.

6. Conduct a post-mortem analysis: After the issue has been resolved and the fix has been deployed, schedule a post-mortem meeting with the team to discuss the root cause, lessons learned, and any process improvements that can be implemented to prevent similar issues in the future.

7. Continuous improvement: Use this incident as an opportunity to identify areas of improvement in the development and testing processes. Evaluate if there are any changes that can be made to prevent similar issues from occurring in the future.

Remember, open communication, collaboration, and continuous learning are key to ensuring the highest quality of your app and maintaining a strong relationship with your clients.

Now, of course, ChatGPT (like every other form of artificial intelligence on the planet) is not entirely perfect. For instance, recommendation number 3 is a valid item to do, except for the fact that it's not usually the responsibility of a QA person to communicate anything directly to the client or customer. That communication can be done either through tech support or with a product manager who has those communication channels (especially if they are a significant customer). So, the suggestion is fine, but it's not appropriate for a person with that role within a company.

Let's Talk About Real Prompt Engineering

If you Google the term "prompt engineering," you'll find a ton of examples, blogs, and even full websites with subscription plans that will try to convince you that the perfect prompts can be created by simply only using text. As you have seen from the examples above, prompt engineering cannot be accomplished solely by merely crafting textual inputs.

In reality, the process is quite similar to cooking a sophisticated meal. Imagine trying to cook, for example, beef bourguignon using only salt as the seasoning, and neglecting all other ingredients and spices! Honestly, the result would pale in comparison to the actual dish.

Similarly, try assembling an entire orchestra but only use one instrument and one musician. That's an embarrassing "one man band." Therefore, simply adjusting the text to the prompt isn't enough in order to truly perform prompt engineering. The parameters such as the model's temperature, which controls randomness; the top-p, impacting token probability; the specific model used; the number of tokens, and the other parameters all play highly pivotal roles in getting a great response.

This book is not about prompt engineering, since (as you can see from the explanation above) it truly involves several factors that don't have anything to do with JavaScript. However, you are highly encouraged to experiment with ALL the parameters to the models provided by OpenAI to find what works best for your use case.

Registering a Slack Bot App

Now that we know the various ways for ChatGPT to summarize a large body of text for us, let's see what's necessary in order to create a simple bot in JavaScript that will programmatically grab all the messages from a channel within a Slack instance.

Note   In order to accomplish these steps, you will need to have administrative access to a Slack workspace. Most developers will **NOT** have these levels of permissions; therefore, in order to fully experiment, I recommend that you create your own personal Slack workspace for testing purposes. This way, you will have all the rights and privileges to install your Slack bot.

But, one step at a time. First, we're going to make our Slack bot app, so head over to the Slack API website:

```
https://api.slack.com/
```

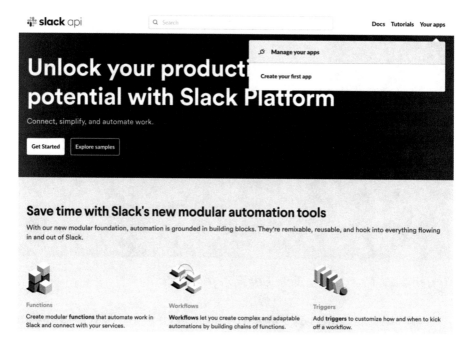

Figure 4-1. *In Order to Create a Slack Bot, Go To the Slack API Website*

Of course, you'll need to have a Slack account in order for this to work, so if you don't have one, then you need to create one first.

After you have logged in, go to the top-right of the page and navigate to "**Your apps ➤ Create your first app**," as shown in Figure 4-1 above. In Slack terminology, a "bot" is an "app," and bots are not allowed to run on a Slack instance unless they have been registered with Slack first.

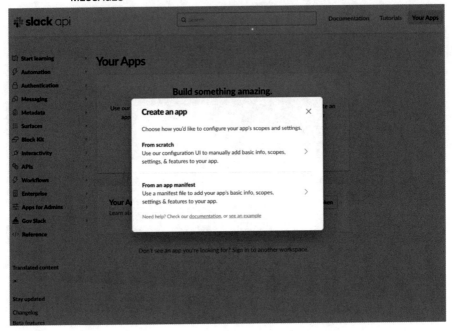

Figure 4-2. *Creating a New Bot App for Slack*

As shown in Figure 4-2, above, you'll be taken to the **Your Apps** page where you can manage your Slack apps. Immediately, you'll see a popup to **Create an App** button in the middle of the screen.

Select the option to create your app **from scratch**. This is because we want to be able to manipulate all of the details of the application ourselves without overcomplicating things with a bunch of default settings.

Afterward, you'll be prompted to specify a name for your bot and to select the workspace that you want your bot to have access to, as shown in Figure 4-3.

Click the **Create App** button to proceed.

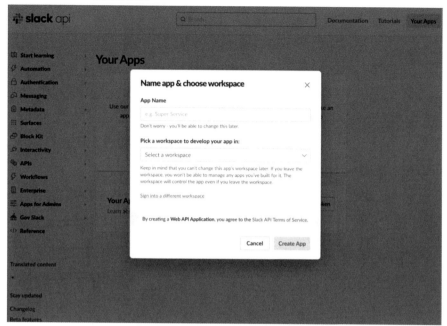

Figure 4-3.   *Creating a New Bot App for Slack*

Specifying What Your Bot Can (and Can't) Do by Setting the Scope

Now, you'll be presented with a screen that has a ton of options for bots for Slack workspaces. The first thing you need to do, however, is from the sidebar on the left, click **OAuth & Permissions**.

Our bot is going to be pretty simple; all it needs to do is read the messages from a channel in order to give us a summary of what was said. In addition to reading the messages, we also need to know the names of the people in the Slack workspace; otherwise, we'll get a UUID representation of the person instead of their name, which is meaningless to us.

So, scroll down and be sure to add the following OAuth Scope to your Slack Bot, as shown in Figure 4-4.

- channels:history

- channels:read

- users:read

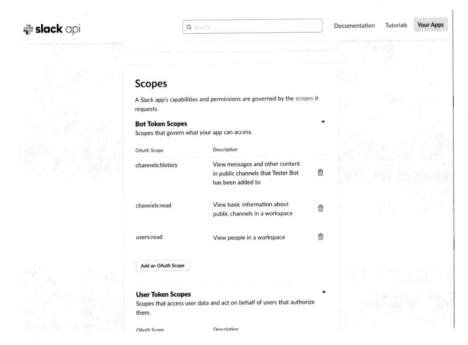

Figure 4-4. *Adding Scopes for the Slack Bot App*

Confirming Your Settings

After you've added the appropriate scopes for your bot, scroll back up and click **Basic Information** from the left side bar.

On the page that follows, you'll see that there's now a green checkmark beside "Add features and functionality," which confirms that you've added your scopes correctly, as shown in Figure 4-5.

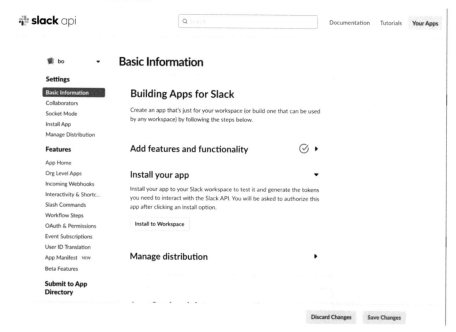

Figure 4-5. *Confirm Your Settings*

Viewing the OAuth & Permissions Page

As shown in Figure 4-6, navigate to the **OAuth & Permissions** page, and click the "Install to Workspace" button.

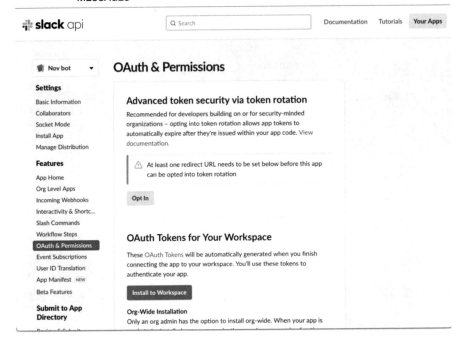

Figure 4-6. *The OAuth & Permission Screen*

Installing Your Slack Bot App to Your Workspace

Now that all the permissions have been requested, it's time to install your bot to your workspace. During the installation process, you should see a screen as shown in Figure 4-7.

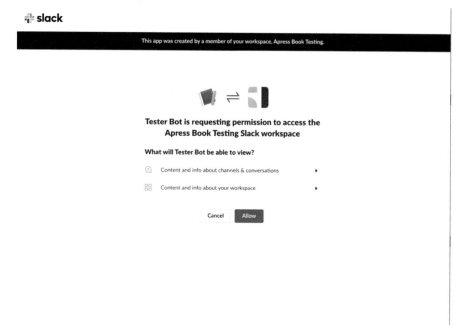

Figure 4-7. *"Installing" a New Slack Bot App*

Click the **Allow** button to authorize the bot and allow the permissions
you allotted in the previous step.

Note   It's important to understand what "installing" means here.
In a traditional JavaScript sense, installing an app means to copy
your code and dependencies over to another machine and have it to
execute. That's not what's happening here.

Here, when you "install" a bot app, you're enabling your Slack
workspace to allow an app to join the workspace – that's all. The code for
your bot will run on your own machine, and not on Slack's servers.

Getting Your Slack Bot (Access) Token

This time, "token" actually means access token! In order to connect to the Slack API and access messages and user information programmatically, you need a specific OAuth token generated for your Slack bot.

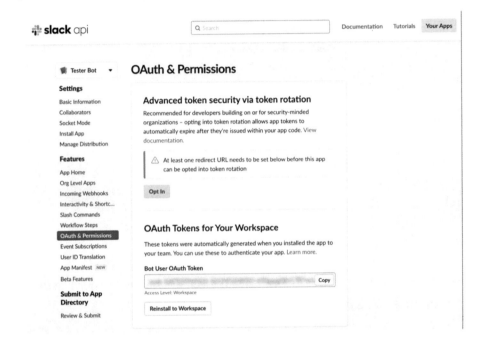

Figure 4-8. *Copy Your OAuth Token for Your Slack Bot App*

Back on the **OAuth & Permissions** page, be sure to copy the bot token (which usually starts with "xoxb-") from the page here, as shown in Figure 4-8.

Inviting Your Bot to Your Channel

Next, you're going to go to the channel you'd like to use to test your bot and type in the following command in the channel itself.

```
/invite
```

Select the option "**Add apps to this channel,**" and then select the
name of the Slack Bot that you specified earlier when you registered the
bot with Slack.

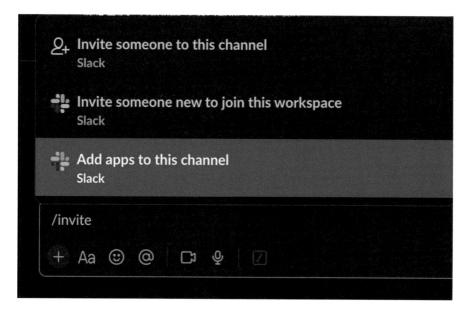

Figure 4-9. Adding Your Slack Bot to a Channel

Congratulations! You now have successfully registered a Slack Bot App
with Slack, enabled it to read messages in your workspace, and added the
Slack Bot to a channel. Before we can write the JavaScript code to access
the channel in our workspace, we need to know what is the internal ID that
Slack uses for our channel.

Finding the Channel ID of Your Channel

Ok, this is an easy step to do. In Slack, right-click the name of your channel
and select the option "**View Channel details.**" At the bottom of the popup
window is the ID of your channel. Copy that number and save it for later.
Your JavaScript app will need this in order to join the right channel in your
Slack workspace.

Using Your Slack Bot App to Automatically Grab Messages from a Channel

Alright, now that we have done all the prerequisites and we know the ID of our channel, let's get to the code in JavaScript that accesses all the messages from a particular Slack channel.

Programmatically Reading Messages from Slack

First things first, you need to install the official JavaScript Slack library. Below is the npm command to install all the necessary dependencies:

```
npm install @slack/web-api @slack/events-api dotenv
```

Listing 4-10 is a simple JavaScript Slack Bot that obtains the user name, timestamp, and message content of each posting in the designated channel.

Listing 4-10. Our JavaScript Slack Bot

```
import { WebClient } from "@slack/web-api";
import "dotenv/config";

const token = process.env.SLACK_API_TOKEN;
const channel_id = process.env.SLACK_CHANNEL_ID;

async function main() {
  const web = new WebClient(token);
  // Store conversation history
  let conversationHistory;
  // ID of channel you watch to fetch the history for

  try {
    // Call the conversations.history method using WebClient
    const result = await web.conversations.history({
```

```
      channel: channel_id,
      limit: 50,
    });

    // Get the messages in the order they were sent.
    conversationHistory = result.messages.reverse();

    // Print results
    for (const message of conversationHistory) {
      const userInfo = await web.users.info({ user: message.
      user });

      // Convert the timestamp into a date
      const timestamp = new Date(parseFloat(message.ts)
      * 1000);

      if (userInfo.ok) {
        console.log(userInfo.user.name + "[" + timestamp + "]"
        + message.text);
        console.log("\n");
      }
    }
  } catch (error) {
    console.error(error);
  }
}

main();
```

Let's walk through this code together.

First, we import essential dependencies required for interfacing with the Slack API and loading environment variables.

Next, we define two crucial variables: the token, which is fetched from the environment variable SLACK_API_TOKEN, and the channel_id, obtained from SLACK_CHANNEL_ID. These variables are necessary for authenticating with the Slack API and specifying the Slack channel's history we want to retrieve.

We then define an asynchronous main function where the core logic of our script resides. Within this function, we initialize the WebClient using our Slack API token to enable API calls. We also declare a variable conversationHistory to store the messages retrieved from the channel.

The premise of the script is simple; it retrieves the last 50 messages from the Slack channel by calling the conversations.history() method of the Slack API.

After successfully fetching the messages, the script reverses their order using .reverse() to ensure they are processed from oldest to newest, and then prints each message.

Listing 4-11 shows the result of running the Slack Bot script.

Listing 4-11. The Output from Executing Our Channel Reader Slack Bot

```
Fatima [2023-08-11T09:04:20] : Hey everyone, I have an urgent
issue to discuss. I just got off a call with a client who's
experiencing app crashes as soon as they load it. They're
really frustrated. Can we get this sorted ASAP? :tired_face:

Keith [2023-08-11T09:04:35] : Thanks for bringing this to our
attention, Fatima. Let's jump on this right away. John, can you
take the lead in investigating the issue since our architect is
out sick today?

John [2023-08-11T09:04:52] : Sure thing, Keith. I'll dive into
the codebase and see if I can find any potential culprits for
the crashes.
```

```
John [2023-08-11T09:05:30] : Fatima, could you gather some
additional information from the client? Ask them about the
specific device, operating system, and any recent updates they
might have installed.

...
```

Exercises Left for the Reader

So, there are obviously a few additional things we can do here, and these steps will be left for you (the reader) to accomplish, for example:

- Connecting the code that reads the messages from Slack to the our ChatGPT client in the previous chapter so that grabbing the messages and getting a summary is a single step process.

- Adding more capabilities to the Slack bot itself such as adding commands so that anyone in the channel can request a summary. In its current state, the bot doesn't post anything in the channel. However, the "user interface" to the bot is the channel itself; therefore, someone should be able to interact with the Slack bot by typing a command (such as requesting a summary).

- Making sure that the bot doesn't make a bad situation worse. Whenever the bot provides a summary, it should not post in the channel itself because that could add a lot of noise to an already noisy situation. The best practice is to have the bot send a private message to the person asking for a summary (or whatever new command that you create).

Conclusion

In this chapter, we talked about one of the various ways artificial intelligence can be put to practical use within the enterprise today. We discussed what is truly "prompt engineering," by discussing that prompt engineering cannot be accomplished by simply textual input to ChatGPT alone. You definitely need to understand the ramifications of all the input parameters to the ChatGPT API, in order to properly, and effectively, perform prompt engineering.

Using what we learned about prompt engineering, we were able to successfully obtain summarizations of any large body of text provided to us. Finally, we saw the code necessary in order to run an automated bot that will grab messages from any Slack channel programmatically.

In this chapter (as well as the previous chapter), we were working exclusively with the Chat Completions Endpoint of the OpenAI APIs. In the next chapter, we're going to push the boundaries of what's possible by experimenting with the Whisper and DALL-E Endpoints.

CHAPTER 5

Multimodal AI: Creating a Podcast Visualizer with Whisper and DALL·E 3

In this chapter, we're going to see the benefits of combining multiple models together in order to create some fascinating results. As an avid podcast listener, I've often wondered what the scenery, the imagery, the characters, the subject, or the background looked like while listening to a very immersive story in audio format.

Let's introduce a new term: **multimodal AI.** In the most simplest of terms, generative AI models can create content in one of four formats:

- Text
- Audio
- Images
- Video

© Bruce Hopkins Jr., Bruce Hopkins Sr. 2025
B. Hopkins Jr. and B. Hopkins Sr., *Creating ChatGPT Apps with JavaScript*,
https://doi.org/10.1007/979-8-8688-1221-7_5

Each of those formats is a **mode**. Multimodal AI is the process of using multiple AI models together to generate (or to understand) content where the input is one type of mode, and the output is a different type of mode.

Take, for example, OpenAI's Whisper model. If you provide it audio, it is able to create a transcription of everything said into text. The same thing applies to DALL·E. If you supply it with a textual prompt, then it can generate an image of what you described.

So we're going to create a Podcast Visualizer using multiple models from OpenAI. There are a few steps involved, but the final results are stunning. While listening to a podcast about a guy cooking some amazing things with tofu (don't knock it until you try it), the Podcast Visualizer came up with the image in Figure 5-1.

Figure 5-1. *AI-Generated Image. The Result of Visualizing a Podcast About Tofu Using the GPT-4, Whisper, and DALL·E Models*

In order to make the code for the Podcast Visualizer easy to follow along, we'll do things separately in the following three steps:

- Step-1: Take a podcast episode and use the Whisper model to get a transcript.

- Step-2: Take the resulting transcript and use the GTP-4 model to describe the visual aspects of what's being discussed in the podcast episode.

- Step-3: Take the resulting description and use the DALL·E model to generate an image.

The code presented here in this chapter has tons of practical uses, for example:

- If you're just curious about what the things in a podcast episode could look like (which is always the case for me), you can get a simple representative visual image to associate with what you're listening to.

- For people who are hearing impaired, you can easily turn a podcast or radio program into a slide-show of images. This greatly enhances the accessibility of the content.

- For podcasters, you can now have a simple way to add a visual/hero image to each of your episodes. This is useful since podcast players such as Apple Podcasts and Spotify allow podcasters to display a single image to associate with an individual episode. This can help with engagement for your listeners.

Introducing the Whisper Model by OpenAI

Now let's introduce another new term: **Automatic Speech Recognition** (ASR). The average everyday consumer is very familiar with this technology due to its integration into mobile phones (e.g., Siri for the iPhone) and smart speakers (e.g., any Alexa device). At its core, ASR technology converts spoken language into text.

Whisper is OpenAI's model for speech recognition, and the accuracy is astonishingly high. The listing below is a transcript of an episode of the very popular DuoLingo Spanish podcast, which makes the Spanish language easy to be understood by English listeners by combining both English and Spanish together in a woven narrative story. The transcript was generated using the Whisper model.

Listing 5-1. The Whisper Model Performs Speech Recognition to Convert Audio into Text

...I'm Martina Castro. Every episode we bring you fascinating, true stories to help you improve your Spanish listening and gain new perspectives on the world. The storyteller will be using intermediate Spanish and I'll be chiming in for context in English. If you miss something, you can always skip back and listen again. We also offer full transcripts at podcast. duolingo.com.

Growing up, Linda was fascinated with her grandmother, Erlinda. Erlinda was a healer or curandera, someone who administers remedies for mental, emotional, physical, or spiritual illnesses.

In Guatemala, this is a practice passed down orally through generations in the same family. Mal de ojo, or the evil eye, is considered an illness by many Guatemalans who believe humans have the power to transfer bad energy to others. Neighbors

```
would bring their babies to Linda's grandmother when they
suspected an energy imbalance. Su madre lo llevaba a nuestra
casa para curarlo...
```

If you've ever worked with a speech recognition system before (even with sophisticated technologies like Siri and Alexa), you will know that it has problems, for instance:

- **Speech recognition has problems with punctuation.**

  - Have you noticed that nobody speaks with punctuation? For the English language, we use changes in tone or volume to ask a question or give an exclamation. We also use short and long pauses for commas and periods.

- **Speech recognition has problems with foreign words and accents.**

  - Depending on who you ask, there are at least 170k words in the English language. However, in conversational English, we are always using foreign words like:

    - Tsunami (Japanese origin): A large sea wave often caused by an earthquake

    - Hors d'oeuvre (French origin): An appetizer

    - Lingerie (French origin): Women's underwear or nightclothes

    - Aficionado (Spanish origin): Someone who is very passionate about a specific activity or subject

    - Piñata (Spanish origin): A brightly colored box of candy for kids to beat relentlessly

- **Speech recognition has problems with names.**

  - Certain names of people, businesses, and websites can often be hard to spell and understand.

- **Speech recognition has problems with homophones.**

  - Do you remember those words that sound the same but have different spellings and meanings? The fantastic editor of this book knows all of them!

    - Would / Wood

    - Flour / Flower

    - Two / Too / To

    - They're / There / Their

    - Pair / Pare / Pear

    - Break / Brake

    - Allowed / Aloud

As you can see from Listing 5-1, Whisper was able to understand all the punctuation in the audio, identify all the foreign words (of which there were several), understand the names, as well as the company name ("Duolingo") within a URL! Of course, if you noticed, it could also understand the difference between "wood" and "would."

Features and Limitations of the Whisper Model

The Whisper model is able to convert spoken audio from the following languages into text:

- Afrikaans

- Arabic

- Armenian

- Azerbaijani

- Belarusian

- Bosnian

- Bulgarian

- Catalan

- Chinese

- Croatian

- Czech

- Danish

- Dutch

- **English (of course!)**

- Estonian

- Finnish

- French

- Galician

- German

- Greek

- Hebrew

- Hindi

- Hungarian

- Icelandic
- Indonesian
- Italian
- Japanese
- Kannada
- Kazakh
- Korean
- Latvian
- Lithuanian
- Macedonian
- Malay
- Marathi
- Maori
- Nepali
- Norwegian
- Persian
- Polish
- Portuguese
- Romanian
- Russian
- Serbian
- Slovak
- Slovenian

- Spanish

- Swahili

- Swedish

- Tagalog

- Tamil

- Thai

- Turkish

- Ukrainian

- Urdu

- Vietnamese

- Welsh

So, at the end of the day, it will be able to understand audio spoken by yourself and probably any language spoken by your friends and colleagues.

Developers are limited to send no more than 50 requests per minute to the API, so this constraint needs to be taken into consideration if you want to transcribe vast amounts of audio.

Whisper supports audio in flac, mp3, mp4, mpeg, mpga, m4a, ogg, wav, or webm formats. Regardless of the format that you use, the maximum file size to send to the API is 25MB.

Now, if you haven't worked extensively with audio files, please be aware that some formats create REALLY HUGE files (e.g., wav format) and others create really small files (e.g., m4a format). So, converting your file to a different format can help you with the 25MB limitation. However, later in this chapter, we'll see the code for a tool that takes a single large audio file and splits it into multiple, smaller files.

Using OpenAI.audio.transcriptions.create() to Transcribe Audio

The OpenAI.audio.transcriptions.create() method converts audio into text and is only compatible with the Whisper model. Let's take a look at what parameters need to be in the method in order to make a successful API call.

Examining the Method Parameters

Table 5-1. *The Request Body for Whisper*

Field	Type	Required?	Description
file	file	Required	The entire audio file that you want to be transcribed.
			Accepted formats are
			• flac
			• mp3
			• mp4
			• mpeg
			• mpga
			• m4a
			• ogg
			• wav
			• webm

(continued)

Table 5-1. (*continued*)

Field	Type	Required?	Description
model	String	Required	The ID of the model that you want to use for transcription.
			Compatible models include
			• whisper-1
prompt	String	Optional	This is any text that can be provided to change the model's transcription style or to provide it with more context from a previous segment of audio.
			Be sure that the prompt is in the same language as the audio for best results.
			Additionally, this field can be used to change the spelling or capitalization of any words that Whisper is not familiar with.
response_ format	String default: json	Optional	This is the format of the output of transcription.
			Accepted formats are
			• json
			• text
			• srt
			• verbose_json
			• vtt

(*continued*)

Table 5-1. (*continued*)

Field	Type	Required?	Description
temperature	Number default: 0	Optional	This is the sampling temperature, ranging from 0 to 1. A higher value increases the randomness of the output, whereas a lower value ensures a more deterministic output.
language	String	Optional	This is the language of the input audio. It's optional, but providing the value can improve the accuracy and latency for the transcription

Creating a Utility App to Split Audio Files

So, we're almost at the point where we are able to programmatically invoke the Whisper model using the Transcriptions Endpoint. However, the Whisper Model has a limitation of 25MB per file.

Now, this is not a problem if you're listening to, for example, the StarDate podcast from the University of Texas at Austin. This podcast gives you a great glimpse of what to look for in the nighttime sky in about 2 minutes of audio. However, that's not the case for other audio programs which tend to last for up to an hour (or even more). In cases like that, you're going to definitely exceed the 25MB file limitation.

Therefore, let's pair-program with ChatGPT and use our human intelligence to create our own utility that will take a single audio file and split it into multiple smaller files.

> **Note**   In this section, I'm presenting one of the many possibilities available on how to segment a large audio file into smaller pieces. For instance, you can use popular audio editing apps (such as the Open Source tool, Audacity, or the licensed tool, Adobe Audition) to manually cut up a large file into smaller files.

FFmpeg is one of the most reliable tools to programmatically manipulate media files, and since it's open source, it's make sense to use it for our needs.

Listing 5-2 is the prompt sums up what we need to get done.

Listing 5-2. PROMPT. Using ChatGPT to Create the AudioSplitter App

System: You are a JavaScript developer

User: Write an application that takes as input a single MP3 file and splits the file into contiguous segments no longer than 10 minutes using the ffmpeg library.

After a little back and forth, I was able to create (as shown in Listing 5-3) the audiosplitter application that includes my edits to what was generated by ChatGPT.

Listing 5-3. RESPONSE. Audio-splitter.js

```
const ffmpeg = require("fluent-ffmpeg");
const ffmpegPath = require("ffmpeg-static");
const path = require("path");
const fs = require("fs");
```

133

```javascript
// Configure ffmpeg to use the static binary
ffmpeg.setFfmpegPath(ffmpegPath);

// Function to split MP3 file
function splitMP3(inputFile, duration) {
  ffmpeg.ffprobe(inputFile, (err, metadata) => {
    if (err) {
      console.error(`Error occurred: ${err.message}`);
      return;
    }

    const totalDuration = metadata.format.duration;
    const numberOfChunks = Math.ceil(totalDuration / duration);
    const outputDir = path.join(__dirname, "output");

    if (!fs.existsSync(outputDir)) {
      fs.mkdirSync(outputDir);
    }

    for (let i = 0; i < numberOfChunks; i++) {
      const startTime = i * duration;
      const outputFile = path.join(outputDir, `output_${i +
1}.mp3`);

      ffmpeg(inputFile)
        .setStartTime(startTime)
        .duration(duration)
        .output(outputFile)
        .on("end", () => {
          console.log(`Created ${outputFile}`);
        })
        .on("error", (err) => {
          console.error(`Error occurred: ${err.message}`);
        })
```

```
        .run();
    }
  });
}

// Usage example
const inputFilePath = path.join(__dirname, "input.mp3"); //
Path to your input MP3 file
const maxDuration = 600; // 10 minutes in seconds

splitMP3(inputFilePath, maxDuration);
```

Our goal is quite simple: split an MP3 file into segments of a specified duration using JavaScript and FFmpeg. Each segment should be no longer than 10 minutes (which is 600 seconds). The entire process is managed using the fluent-ffmpeg library, which acts as a Node.js wrapper for FFmpeg, allowing us to handle audio and video processing efficiently.

Of course, one of the first steps required is to ensure that you have FFmpeg installed and correctly configured. Our script uses ffmpeg-static to ensure the FFmpeg binary is packaged with the code. This avoids system-specific dependency issues. You can install your dependencies with the following command:

```
npm install fluent-ffmpeg ffmpeg-static
```

The main logic resides in the splitMP3() function, which takes two arguments: the path to the input MP3 file and the desired segment duration (in seconds).

First, we use the ffmpeg.ffprobe() function to extract metadata from the input MP3 file, specifically its total duration. This is necessary because it lets us determine how many segments we need to create.

If the output directory does not exist, we create it using Node.js's fs module. This ensures that our segmented audio files have a dedicated destination folder.

After running the script, the output folder will be populated with MP3 files, each no longer than 10 minutes in duration. If the input file is less than 10 minutes, only one segment will be generated.

Creating the Audio Transcriber with Whisper

Now, let's build our next JavaScript app, which will use the Whisper model to create transcriptions of audio. Again, we're going to pair-program with ChatGPT to get a basis to work with.

Listing 5-4 is the prompt to put in the Chat Playground to get things started. Be sure to note that I'm asking for a 60-sec HTTP request timeout since Whisper may take a little while to generate the transcript.

Listing 5-4. PROMPT: Asking ChatGPT to Use OpenAI's JavaScript Library and Send MP3 Files to Whisper's API

System: You are a JavaScript developer.

User: Using JavaScript, write a script that iterates over all of the mp3 files in a single folder on my local computer and send all the files in the folder to the webservice provided by OpenAI's Whisper model, using the OpenAI's node.js library.

Model: gpt-4

Temperature: 1

Maximum Length: 1150

After some back and forth, here's the response ChatGPT gave us that worked (Listing 5-5):

Listing 5-5. RESPONSE: WhispeR TRANSCRIBER Script

```
const fs = require("fs");
const path = require("path");
const { OpenAI } = require("openai");

// Set up the OpenAI client with your API key
const openai = new OpenAI({
  apiKey: process.env.OPENAI_API_KEY,
});

// Function to read and transcribe .mp3 files in a directory
async function transcribeMP3Files(directory) {
  try {
    // Read the directory
    const files = fs.readdirSync(directory);

    // Filter out .mp3 files
    const mp3Files = files.filter((file) => path.extname(file)
    === ".mp3");

    // Process each .mp3 file
    for (const file of mp3Files) {
      const filePath = path.join(directory, file);

      // Read the .mp3 file
      const fileData = fs.readFileSync(filePath);

      // Send the file to OpenAI's Whisper
      const response = await openai.transcriptions.create({
        file: fileData,
```

```
      model: "whisper-1",
    });

    // Output the transcription
    console.log(`Transcription for ${file}:`);
    console.log(response.data.text);
    }
  } catch (error) {
    console.error("Error processing files:", error);
  }
}

// Set the directory to read from
const directoryPath = "./mp3-files";

// Run the transcription function
transcribeMP3Files(directoryPath);
```

Having a Little Fun and Trying Things Out with a Podcast

Ok, so let's run a test using the code that we have presented so far. "This American Life" is a weekly public radio program (and also a podcast) that's hosted by Ira Glass and produced in collaboration with WBEZ Chicago.

Each episode weaves together a series of stories centered around a specific theme or topic. Some stories are investigative journalism, and others are simply interviews with ordinary people with captivating stories. Episode 811 is entitled, "The one place I can't go," and the file is 56MB in MP3 format. Since we already know that 56MB is way too big to send to Whisper to get transcribed, let's run our tools to break up the audio file and transcribe the individual segments.

Listing 5-6 shows an excerpt from the full transcript of the episode.

Listing 5-6. The Partial Transcript of Episode 811 of This American Life

"...My younger cousin Camille is not really a dog person, but there is one dog she adored. Her name was Foxy, because she looked exactly like a fox, except she was black. She was the neighbor's dog, but she and Camille seemed to have a real kinship, maybe because they both weren't very far from the ground. Camille was around four or five years old back then, and she had a little lisp, so Foxy came out as Fozzie. I thought it was one of the cutest things I'd ever heard.

The way Camille remembers Foxy, it's almost like a movie. Her memories feel like endless summer, hazy and perfect, like a scene shot on crackly film. I just remembered like the feeling of being excited to go and see Foxy. I have an image in my head of like coming to the house, and I could see Foxy was like outside. I can see Foxy through the door that leads to the garden. There's a story about Camille and Foxy that I think about fairly often. I've talked about it with my sister for years, but never with Camille. And it's this. Once when they were playing..."

For brevity, we're only showing an excerpt of the transcript. The full transcript itself is over 8000 words due to the fact that the episode is nearly 1 hr in length.

Going Meta: Prompt Engineering gpt-4o-mini to Write a Prompt for DALL·E

Since the full text transcript of the podcast episode that we want to visualize is thousands of words, we're going to use gpt-4o-mini to automatically create the prompt needed for the DALL·E model. DALL·E is able to take a textual description in a prompt and create an image, but it's best to keep the prompt as short as possible. Listing 5-7 is the prompt for gpt-4o-mini to generate a prompt for DALL·E.

Listing 5-7. The Prompt for GPT-4 to Create a Prompt for DALL·E

System: You are a service that helps to visualize podcasts.

User: Read the following transcript from a podcast. Describe for a visually impaired person the background and subject that best represents the overall theme of the episode. Start with any of the following phrases:
- "A photo of"
- "A painting of"
  "A macro 35mm photo of"
  "Digital art of "

User: Support for This American Life comes from Squarespace...

Model: gpt-4o-mini

Temperature: 1.47

Maximum length: 150

Top P: 0

Frequency penalty: 0.33

Presence penalty: 0

140

As you can see in the prompt, the model used is the gpt-4o-mini which allows us to process REALLY LONG text transcripts of 128k tokens. DALL·E needs to know the type of image to generate so that's why we need to specify that the image should be a photo, painting, digital art, etc. We need to ensure that the resulting text generated by the model is short, so we want to have a maximum length of 150 tokens. Also, in order to prevent ChatGPT from repeating some phrases multiple times, we introduced a frequency penalty of 0.33.

Listing 5-8 shows the results from ChatGPT after reading the transcript of Episode 811 of This American Life.

Listing 5-8. The Prompt for DALL·E Created by GPT-4o-mini

```
Digital art of a young girl sitting in a garden with a black
dog that looks like a fox. The girl is smiling and the dog is
wagging its tail. The image has a hazy, dream-like quality,
with crackly film effects to evoke nostalgia.
```

Using OpenAI.openai.images.generate() to Create Images

The OpenAI.images.generate() method allows you to use the DALL·E model to dynamically create an image from a text prompt.

Table 5-2 describes the format of the JSON object necessary to create images. For obvious reasons, the prompt itself is the only required parameter in order to successfully invoke the service.

Create Image (JSON)

Table 5-2. *Request Body for the Create Image Endpoint*

Field	Type	Required?	Description
prompt	String	Required	This is where you describe the image that you want to be created.
			The maximum length is 1000 characters for dall-e-2 and 4000 characters for dall-e-3.
model	String Default: "dall-e-2"	Optional	The model name to generate the image. Compatible models include • "dall-e-2" • "dall-e-3"
n	integer or null Default: 1	Optional	This is the requested number of images that you want created. Must be between 1 and 10. Note: Due to the complexity required for dall-e-3, OpenAI may limit your request to a single image
quality	String Default: "standard"	Optional	This allows you to specify the quality of the image to be generated. This parameter is only valid for dall-e-3. Accepted values are • "standard" • "hd"

(*continued*)

Table 5-2. (*continued*)

Field	Type	Required?	Description
size	String or null Default: "1024x1024"	Optional	The size of the generated images. Image sizes available for dall-e-2 are • "256x256" • "512x512" • "1024x1024" Image sizes available for dall-e-3 are • "1024x1024" • "1792x1024" (landscape) • "1024x1792" (portrait)
style	String Default: "vivid"	Optional	This allows you to specify how natural looking the generated image should be. This parameter is only valid for dall-e-3. Accepted values are • "natural" (good for photos) • "vivid" (good for artistic looks)
response_ format	String or null Default: "url"	Optional	This is the format of the generated image. Accepted values are • "url" • "b64_json"
user	String	Optional	This is a unique identifier representing your end-user, which can help OpenAI to monitor and detect abuse.

Handling the Response

After successfully invoking the method, the API will respond with an Image JSON object. Here's a breakdown of the Image object, which only has one parameter (Table 5-3).

Image

Table 5-3. *The Structure of the Image Object*

Field	Type	Description
url (or) b64_json	String	This is a url to your generated image if the response_ format is "url" in the request.
		(or)
		This is a base64-encoded JSON image if the response_ format is "b64_json" in the request.

Creating the Images with the DALL·E Model

As you can see from Tables 5-2 and 5-3, the creating an image with the DALL·E model is a very straightforward process. Therefore, our code in Listing 5-9 shows how to create images programmatically in JavaScript.

Listing 5-9. Using the DALL·E Model to Create Images with JavaScript

```javascript
const { OpenAI } = require("openai");
require("dotenv").config();

async function main() {
  // Set up the OpenAI client with your API key
  const openai = new OpenAI({
```

144

```
    apiKey: process.env.OPENAI_API_KEY,
  });

  const response = await openai.images.generate({
    model: "dall-e-3",
    n: 1,
    // The prompt and for the image
    prompt:
      "a 35mm macro photo of 3 cute Rottweiler puppies with no
      collars laying down in a field",
    size: "1024x1024",
  });
  image_url = response.data[0].url;
  console.log(image_url);
}

main();
```

Alright, let's break down what's happening in this code example. We're using the openai.images.generate() function from OpenAI's API to generate an image based on our prompt.

- A prompt is defined. In this case, the prompt describes the desired image: "a 35mm macro photo of 3 cute Rottweiler puppies with no collars laying down in a field."

- The desired size of the generated image is specified as "1024x1024".

- The openai.images.generate() function is called with the provided prompt, size, and model parameters. This function generates an image based on the input prompt using the specified model ("dall-e-3").

- The response object (called an ImageResponse) contains information about the generated image, including its URL.

- Finally, the code prints out the URL of the generated image.

In summary, this code generates an image of three cute Rottweiler puppies laying down in a field based on the provided prompt using the DALL·E model, and then it prints out the URL where the generated image can be accessed.

Visualizing the Podcast

Now that we have the code necessary to create images with the DALL·E model, Figure 5-2 shows the images generated from the text prompt in Listing 5-8 shown earlier.

Figure 5-2. *AI-Generated Image. The DALL·E Generated Image of a Girl and Her Dog from Episode 811 of "This American Life" Podcast*

DALL·E Prompt Engineering and Best Practices

Now, creating images with DALL·E takes prompt engineering in order to get consistent, desired results, and it's a good idea to play around with different prompts to get some practice to see what works for you and your use case. Maybe you prefer paintings instead of 3D looking images? Maybe you need photos instead of digital art? Maybe you want the image to be a close-up shot instead of a portrait? There's a lot of possibilities to consider.

147

Regardless of your use case, here are two golden rules in order to get the most out of your DALL·E prompts.

DALL·E Golden Rule #1: Get Familiar with the Types of Images That DALL·E Can Generate

First and foremost, one of the most important things that DALL·E needs to understand is the type of image that needs to be generated. Here's a list of several of the most common types of images that DALL·E is able to create:

- 3-D render
- Painting
- Abstract painting
- Expressive oil painting
- Oil painting (in the style of any deceased artist)
- Oil pastel
- Digital art
- Photo
- Photorealistic
- Hyperrealistic
- Neon photo
- 35-mm macro photo
- High-quality photo
- Silhouette
- Vaporware

- Cartoon

- Plush object

- Marble sculpture

- Hand sketch

- Poster

- Pencil and watercolor

- Synth wave

- Comic book style

- Hand drawn

DALL·E Golden Rule #2: Be Descriptive with What You Want in the Foreground and Background

I cannot emphasize enough that you need to be descriptive with DALL·E in order to get consistent, desirable results. It may sound weird, but the best way to describe your image to DALL·E is to act like you're describing a dream to another person.

So, as a mental exercise between us, try to describe your last dream. As you describe the people, places, and things in your dream, you have in your mind the most important things that you remember, as well as the experience that you felt. As you describe things to another person, tiny details start to emerge such as

- How many people were present (if any)?

- What position were the people or animals in? Standing, sitting, or laying down?

- What things were in the scenery and the background?

- What items stood out to you? Sounds? Smells? Colors?

- How did you feel? Happy, eerie, excited?

- What was the perceived time of day? Morning, midday, night?

If you can describe a dream to another person, then you should have no problem describing what you want to DALL·E.

Conclusion

In this chapter, we accomplished a lot! With a few scripts, we created a Podcast Visualizer.

- We created and used the audio-splitter script, which works as a utility for us. If you have an audio file that's larger than the limitations of the Whisper model, this script will give you a folder of smaller audio files to send to Whisper.

- We created a script to use the audio-splitter and send the folder of files to Whisper for transcription. Your only limitation is the number of requests that you can send to the Whisper model.

- We did a little prompt engineering in order to get a descriptive prompt of the imagery in a podcast based upon the transcript.

- Finally, we created and used the DALLE-model to take the prompt generated from calling the gpt-4-o-mini model and getting an image that represents the podcast episode visually.

Exercises Left for the Reader

So, there are obviously a few additional things we can do here, and these steps will be left for you (the reader) to accomplish, for example:

- The audio-splitter script our JavaScript interface to FFmpeg. FFmpeg can not only split audio files, but can also do a lot more with media files, such as format conversion and reencoding. Experiment to see which of the supported media formats by Whisper are the smallest audio files. Hint: It's definitely not WAV format.

  If you're planning to create an app or a service that automatically generates images based upon a textual prompt from your end users, then you definitely would want to update the DALL-E script in order to ensure that you're tracking and providing in your request the user parameter. This is due to the fact that your end user has the potential to generate harmful images through your API key. Remember, you have an API account with Open AI, and they don't! As a result, you need to be aware if you need to terminate your business relationship with a user who is violating Open AI content rules through your service.

CHAPTER 6

Creating an Automated Community Manager Bot with Discord and JavaScript

When you're launching an app or a service, it's important to build and maintain your own community. Below are the telltale signs of a healthy user community:

- Members engage in meaningful discussions, sharing insights, feedback, and support.

- Disagreements or debates occur, but they are approached constructively without resorting to personal attacks or derogatory language.

- There's an atmosphere of respect, where members listen to each other and acknowledge differing opinions.

© Bruce Hopkins Jr., Bruce Hopkins Sr. 2025
B. Hopkins Jr. and B. Hopkins Sr., *Creating ChatGPT Apps with JavaScript*,
https://doi.org/10.1007/979-8-8688-1221-7_6

- A mix of old and new members actively participate, ensuring the community remains vibrant and doesn't stagnate.

- Users contribute diverse content, from answering questions to sharing resources, which enriches the community's knowledge base.

- There's a balance between giving and taking; members who seek help or information also offer it to others.

- New members frequently join, often referred by existing members, indicating that the community is seen positively and worth recommending.

- Users often become advocates for the community or platform, promoting it outside of the direct community space, such as on social media or other forums.

- The community helps to shape the app or service by providing new ideas for features and functionality.

No matter what type of app or service that we create, we would love for our user community to exemplify the items listed above!

Choosing Discord as Your Community Platform

Over the past few years, Discord has surged in popularity as a useful tool for community management for people who are passionate about their communities. This is partially due to its cross-platform compatibility, allowing members to stay connected whether they're on a desktop, mobile device, or web browser. However, one of its standout features is the invitation-based community system, which helps community managers to

154

control growth and prevents spam. This model not only ensures a tailored experience for members but also enhances security, since community managers have the discretion to grant or deny access.

Discord not only supports text messaging but also supports voice chats and streaming video. Very similar to Slack, Discord allows community managers to separate content into channels to organize discussions, streamline information flow, and to help users see the content that they're interested in.

Creating a More Advanced Bot Than Our Slack Bot

Now, If you successfully went through the steps in Chapter 4 where we worked with a Slack bot, then the steps in this chapter will feel familiar to you. In Chapter 4, we created a Slack bot to read a single channel during a time period and get a summary of the content discussed. The Slack bot was not a community manager, but was more like a helpful assistant.

For the remainder of this book, we're going to perform all the steps necessary to make powerful bots for Discord that will use AI to help actually manage the community.

Creating a More Advanced Bot Than Any Typical Discord Bot

If you've ever had any experience using a Discord bot, then you're probably aware that the most common way in order to interact with them is with what's called a "/command". This enables typical bots (read: non-intelligent bots) to essentially work only when they have received a very specific operation or command. If the "/command" is not provided, then the bot will be silent and not do anything. Essentially, it exemplifies the phrase, "speak only when you are spoken to."

However, we are creating a Discord bot that will be artificially intelligent, and therefore it will be much more advanced than any typical Discord bot. We're going to create bots that will be able to read and see all messages in the Discord server and be intelligent enough to respond correctly.

Understanding the Roles for the Bots

So let's explore a scenario in order to make things real. We're creating a public Discord server to interact with the users of a mobile banking app. Our end goal is to have bots written in JavaScript to handle the following scenarios:

- Q&A: Monitor a specific channel and automatically answer questions from users about how to use the banking app. For this to work, the bot will need to be trained on how the app works.

- No Solicitations: For any business community, it's important that the participants of the community are not being targeted by unscrupulous individuals. For example, if you're creating a banking app, do you want your customers contacted by anyone whose username is "B4nk Admin"?

- No Harmful Content: For any community, it's important for the members to be protected from harmful content such as hate language.

Our Example Bank: Crook's Bank

For the purposes of this example, we decided upon a fictional name of a fictional bank that would have an extremely low likelihood of coinciding with the name of a real bank. Therefore, for this example, "Crook's Bank" is launching a new mobile app for customers of their bank. They want to have a channel that will be monitored by a bot to answer questions from users of the app, and they also want to ensure that no one is soliciting users of their app, or posting hurtful or harmful content in their Discord servers.

Figure 6-1. *This fake App from a Fake Bank has real problems*

First Things First: Create Your Own Discord Server

Before we can make an AI Discord Bot, we're obviously going to need a Discord server already in place for the bot to interact with. Use either the Discord App or go to the Discord website (login first of course) and start the process to Add/Create a new server.

After you have started the process, select the option labeled, "**Create My Own**" as shown in Figure 6-2.

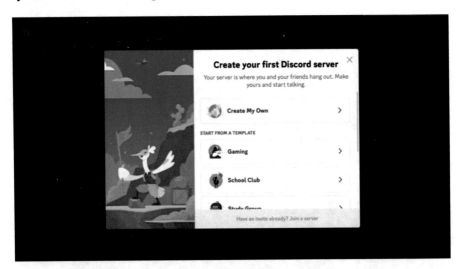

Figure 6-2. *Creating Your Own Discord Server*

Next, you'll be prompted to specify additional information about your server. Continue to proceed through the creation process until you are prompted to provide a name and icon for your server, as shown in Figure 6-3.

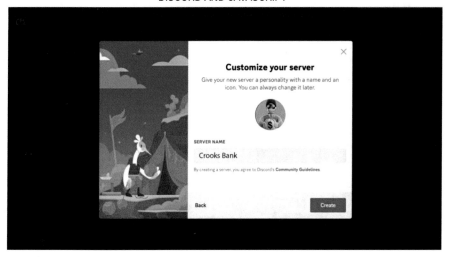

Figure 6-3. *Providing a Name for Your Own Discord Server*

Specify the name of your server and provide an optional server icon (if you have one).

Create the Q&A Channel

By default, every Discord server has a "general" channel, but we want a dedicated channel especially for questions and answers. Depending upon how you created your server, Figures 6-4 and 6-5 will be presented to you to create your new channel.

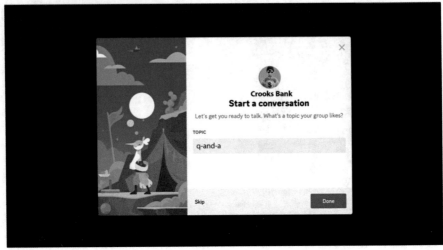

Figure 6-4. *Creating a Channel Using the Web Interface*

Figure 6-5. *Creating a Channel Using the discord App*

Registering a New Discord Bot App with Discord

Now that we have our Discord server with the appropriate channels created, it's time to register the bot itself – or rather, in our case, the bots themselves. In order to keep the code clean and manageable, we'll actually have multiple bots for our Discord server. The first bot will be used exclusively to answer questions in the "q-and-a" channel. The second bot will monitor all channels for unwanted content, such as harmful content or solicitations.

In order to create our bot, head over to the Discord Developers website:

https://discord.com/developers

At the top-right of the page, click the button "**New Application**," as shown in Figure 6-6.

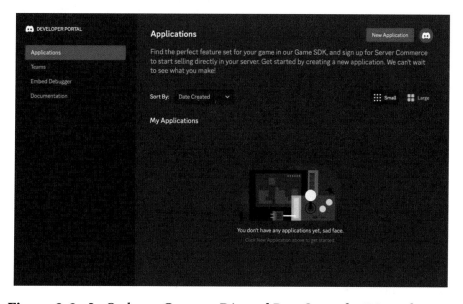

Figure 6-6. *In Order to Create a Discord Bot, Go to the Discord Developer Website*

In both Discord and Slack terminology, a "bot" is an "app," and bots are not allowed to run on Discord servers unless they have been registered with Discord first.

Specify a name for the bot and click the "**Create**" button, as shown in Figure 6-7.

Figure 6-7. *Creating/Registering a Bot for Discord*

Specifying General Info for the Bot

Afterward, you will be taken to a page where you can specify general information about your bot, as shown in Figure 6-8.

Be sure to familiarize yourself with the navigation menu on the left side of the page. As you can see, we have several categories of settings to configure for our bot. By default, we have landed on the "**General Information**" page, where we specify basic info about our bot. If you have an icon ready for your bot, you can upload it here.

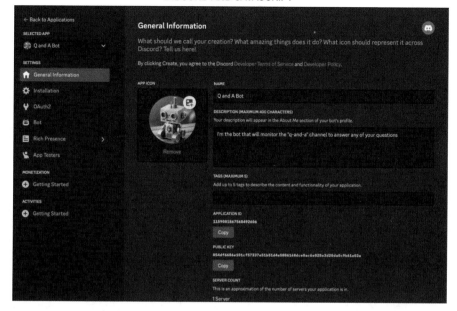

Figure 6-8. *We Decided to Give Our Bot a Cute Little Robot Icon*

Specifying OAuth2 Parameters for the Bot

Now it's time to specify the scopes and permissions for our bot. If you
followed the steps in creating a Slack bot in Chapter 4, then (as stated
before) this procedure will feel familiar to you. Bots **cannot** and **should
not** have the ability to do anything and everything – they should be only
allowed to perform a list of operations that they were designed to perform.

On the settings navigation menu on the left, navigate to "**OAuth2 ➤
URL Generator**" to continue.

Below are the scopes that we want:

- Scopes
  - Bot

This is reflected in Figure 6-9.

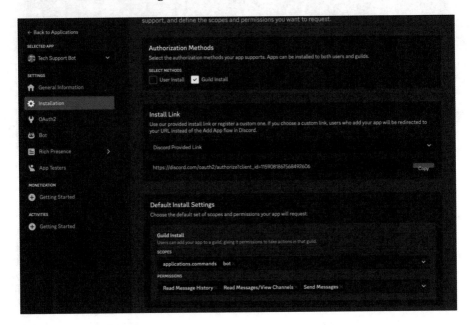

Figure 6-9. *Selecting the Scopes*

After we select the bot's scope, we get to see all the permissions that are only applicable to bots, listed in alphabetical order.

Bots can be pretty powerful depending on the permissions you give it. There are permissions that allow the bot to act in the capacity of a normal human moderator, such as managing the server, roles, and channels. Bots with these permissions can also kick and ban members.

What we're going to enable for our bot right now are the ones that allow the bot to send and receive messages in text channels. This is what we need. Although we're not doing anything special right now with audio, we could enable voice permissions to allow the bot to participate in voice channels. Simple enough, right?

Select the following permissions for the bot:

- Bot Permissions

  - Read Message History

  - Read Messages/View Channels

  - Send Messages

Although you haven't written any JavaScript code yet, now it's time to
invite your bot to your server.

Invite Your Bot to Your Server

As shown in Figure 6-9, after you have selected the appropriate
permissions, Discord will give you a dynamically generated URL that will
enable you to invite your bot to your server.

Copy the URL and paste it into a web browser where you're already
authenticated into Discord. The result is shown in Figure 6-10.

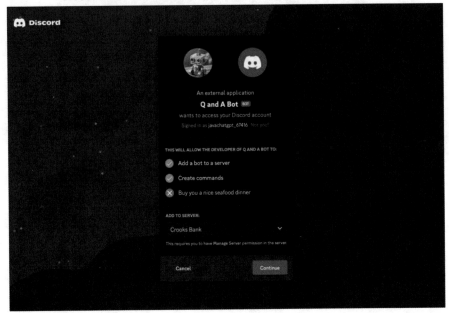

Figure 6-10. *If You Read the Screen Carefully Here, You Can See That Discord Has a Sense of Humor*

Click the "**Continue**" button to add the bot to your server.

Next, you will see a page that looks quite similar to the previous one, but the main difference is that it will give you a summary of all the permissions and capabilities of the bot. Typically this is quite useful if you are adding a bot to a server that you DID NOT CREATE. However, since we created this bot ourselves, this is just a confirmation of the settings that we have already specified earlier (Figure 6-11).

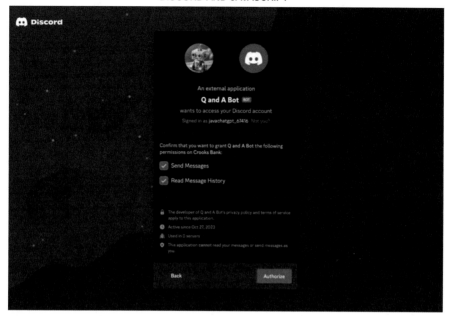

Figure 6-11.   *Confirming the capabilities of the bot*

Click the "**Authorize**" button to give the bot the permission to run on your server.

If everything went smoothly, then you should see an automated message in the General channel of your server that indicates that the process has been successful.

Getting the Discord ID Token for Your Bot and Setting the Gateway Intents

Now it's time to get the Discord ID token for your bot, which you'll use in your code to authenticate your bot programmatically.

Note   For obvious reasons, using the word "token" here makes me nervous because this word has two distinct meanings in this book due to the context, but here's a quick refresher on the meanings:

- When using Discord and Slack APIs, a "token" is an authentication token.

- When using OpenAI APIs, a "token" is a part of a word.

Go back to the Discord developer's website and click the "**Bot**" category in the settings navigation menu to continue.

Although you haven't seen your token yet, you need to click on the "Reset Token" button, as shown in Figure 6-12.

Be sure to copy and save the ID token to someplace safe. You will need this token in the JavaScript code that's presented later in this chapter.

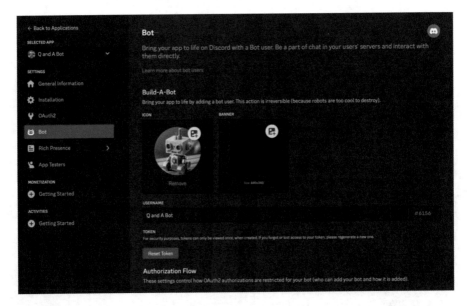

Figure 6-12. *Click the "reset Token" button to see your ID Token*

Scroll down the page to the section named, "**Privileged Gateway Intents**," and enable the option named, "**MESSAGE CONTENT INTENT**."

Note   So let's slow things down a bit and talk about intents. What exactly is an "intent" and why is it needed? For the purposes of the Discord API, you need to specify explicitly every type of information that you want to be notified by Discord programmatically. Otherwise, Discord will constantly bombard you with events that are not relevant to you or your bot. For example, for our purposes, we don't care when people join or leave the server. However, if you want to send a list of server rules to anyone who joins your server for the first time, then you definitely would want to enable the "**SERVER MEMBERS INTENT**." When we deep dive into the code, you'll see more information about intents.

Be sure to click the green button, "**Save Changes**," to save your changes. The result is shown in Figure 6-13.

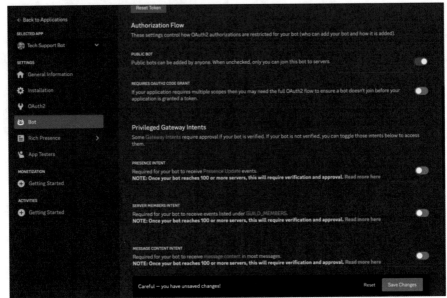

Figure 6-13. *Enable the option named, "MESSAGE CONTENT INTENT"*

Creating a Q&A Bot App in JavaScript to Answer Questions from a Channel

Of course, now that we've done all the prerequisites necessary and we know the name of the channel that we want to monitor for questions from our users, let's get to the code in JavaScript that joins our server and accesses all the messages from a specific Discord channel.

This is the first of two Discord bots that we're creating in this chapter. This bot will be responsible for watching the messages in the "q-and-a" channel in our Discord server.

Later on in this chapter, we'll create another bot that will be responsible for moderating ALL CONTENT in the Discord server for unwanted content, including the "q-and-a" channel. The goal here is follow the architectural pattern of "separation of concerns." Rather than creating a gigantic JavaScript Discord bot that performs all the moderation needs for the Discord server, we're going to separate the functionality into two different apps.

We're also going to take things step by step and focus this chapter on getting past the learning curve for the Discord capabilities in JavaScript. In the final chapters of this book, we'll enhance both bots and make them artificially intelligent using the Open AI APIs.

Listing 6-1 is the code that we need to create a basic Discord bot that watches all the messages posted in a single channel and provides an answer.

Listing 6-1. Our Simplified Tech Support Bot

```javascript
// Require the necessary discord.js classes
const { Client, Events, GatewayIntentBits } =
require("discord.js");
require("dotenv").config();

// Configuration variables
const CHANNEL_NAME = "q-and-a";
const CUSTOM_STATUS = "Ready to answer your questions";

// Create a new client instance
const client = new Client({
  intents: [
    GatewayIntentBits.MessageContent,
    GatewayIntentBits.GuildMessages,
    GatewayIntentBits.Guilds,
  ],
});

client.once(Events.ClientReady, (readyClient) => {
  console.log(`Ready! Logged in as ${readyClient.user.tag}`);
```

```javascript
  // Set the custom status
  client.user.setActivity(CUSTOM_STATUS);
});

client.on(Events.MessageCreate, async (message) => {
    if (client.user.username === message.author.username) return;
    if (message.channel.name !== CHANNEL_NAME) return;

    console.log("User is:", message.author.globalName || message.
    author.username);
    console.log("Message is:", message.content);

    const reply = `${mention(message.author)}, I can help you
    with that!`;
    await message.channel.send(reply);
});

function mention(author) {
  return `<@${author.id}>`;
}

// Log in to Discord with your client's token
client.login(process.env.DISCORD_BOT_API_TOKEN);
```

Now let's delve into the code in Listing 6-1 to understand how our simplified tech support bot works. This bot is designed to monitor messages in the "q-and-a" channel of your Discord server and provide responses to the users' questions.

Note   For some reason, Discord's own terminology sometimes refers to Discord servers as "guilds." However, from our perspective, a guild is simply a Discord server.

Creating the Discord Client

It's pretty easy to create a Discord client using a few lines of code:

```
// Create a new client instance
const client = new Client({
  intents: [
    GatewayIntentBits.MessageContent,
    GatewayIntentBits.GuildMessages,
    GatewayIntentBits.Guilds,
  ],
});
```

Here, we instantiate a new Discord client and provide an intents array
to tell Discord which events we want our bot to receive, namely:

- MessageContent: Allows the bot to read the content of
  messages

- GuildMessages: Enables the bot to receive messages
  from the Discord server.

- Guilds: Allows the bot to receive updates about Discord
  server it's a part of

Listening for New Messages in Our Preferred Discord Channel

Obviously, the most important function here in our bot is the client.on()
event listener, which we use to monitor every new message posted in the
Discord server.

```
client.on(Events.MessageCreate, async (message) => {
  if (client.user.username === message.author.username) return;
  if (message.channel.name !== CHANNEL_NAME) return;
```

```
console.log("User is:", message.author.globalName || message.
author.username);
console.log("Message is:", message.content);

const reply = `${mention(message.author)}, I can help you
with that!`;
await message.channel.send(reply);
});
```

If a message comes from the "q-and-a" channel, our bot will send a friendly (albeit, non-helpful at the moment) response to the sender. As a nice little touch, the author is tagged in the reply so they can be notified when the response is posted.

Success! Running Your First Discord Bot

Now let's run our JavaScript Discord bot. After executing the script, be sure to return back to your Discord server and try to type a question in the channel that you setup for Q&A. Figure 6-14 shows the response to the question, "Is this bot going to answer my questions about the app?"

Figure 6-14. *Success running the Q&A Bot in discord*

As you carefully inspect Figure 6-14, you'll see some key
features such as

- On the right side, you'll see that the bot is online with a
  green status indicator.

- The bot also has a custom status to let you know what it
  will do in the channel.

- After asking a question in the channel, the bot will tag
  you directly.

Streamlining the Process of Registering Our Next Discord Bot App

Now that we have successfully performed all the steps in order to get a
functioning Discord bot, creating the second bot will be a piece of cake!
So, let's briefly reiterate all the steps from above in order to create our
second Discord bot. We'll be sure to point out the items that need to be
changed or enhanced due to the fact that this second bot will work as a
moderator, instead of providing answers to questions from the users of our
Discord server.

Registering a New Discord Bot App with Discord

Perform the same steps as above; however, it would be wise to give the
bot a different name. For our purposes, this second bot will be named,
"Content Mod Bot."

Specifying General Info for the Bot

We decided to have a different icon for the Content Moderator bot, so we specified it here (Figure 6-15).

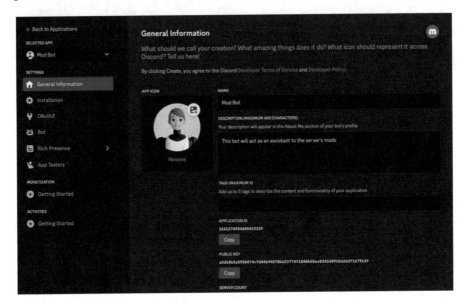

Figure 6-15. *Providing a Name and Icon for the Second Bot*

Specifying OAuth2 Parameters for the Bot

This second bot needs more permissions in order to perform more tasks. Below are the scopes that we want:

- Bot

  - Kick Members

  - Ban Members

  - Send Messages

  - Manage Messages

  - Read Message History

Invite Your Bot to Your Server

Repeat the same steps as above for the first bot.

Getting the Discord ID Token for Your Bot and Setting the Gateway Intents

Again, follow the steps above in order to get the Discord ID Token. Then scroll down the page to the section named, "**Privileged Gateway Intents**" and enable the options named, "**SERVER MEMBERS INTENT**" and "**MESSAGE CONTENT INTENT**."

Creating the Next Discord Bot, the Content Moderator

The role of the content moderator is to make sure that unwanted content is not posted in the Discord server. Just like the previous bot that we created earlier in this chapter, this bot will not (yet) be artificially intelligent. In its current state, the bot will indiscriminately delete any message posted anywhere in the server that contains the word, "puppies."

It's not because puppies are inherently evil. However, they do have a tendency to destroy your favorite pair of shoes when left alone. In all honesty, we simply need something to test our code in Discord when we run our bot.

Listing 6-2 is the code for this simplified Content Moderator.

Listing 6-2. Our Simplified Content Moderator Bot

```javascript
// Require the necessary discord.js classes
const { Client, Events, GatewayIntentBits } =
require("discord.js");
require("dotenv").config();

// Create a new client instance
const client = new Client({
  intents: [
    GatewayIntentBits.MessageContent,
    GatewayIntentBits.GuildMessages,
    GatewayIntentBits.Guilds,
  ],
});

const BANNED_WORD = "puppies";

client.once(Events.ClientReady, (readyClient) => {
  console.log(`Ready! Logged in as ${readyClient.user.tag}`);
});

client.on(Events.MessageCreate, async (message) => {
  if (client.user.username === message.author.username) return;

  if (message.content.includes(BANNED_WORD)) {
    if (!(await message.delete())) {
      console.log("Failed to delete message");
    } else {
      const authorMention = `${mention(message.author)}`;
      const reply = `${authorMention} This comment was deemed
      inappropriate for this channel.\nIf you believe this
      to be in error, please contact one of the human server
      moderators.`;
```

```
      await message.channel.send(reply);
    }
  }
});

function mention(author) {
  return `<@${author.id}>`;
}

client.login(process.env.DISCORD_BOT_API_TOKEN);
```

Handling Messages Sent to the Discord Server

Again, let's focus our attention on the client.on() event listener function,
since it's called asynchronously every time a message is posted to the
Discord server. As you can see, if the message posted to the server contains
the banned word, then we delete the message, and warn the sender with
a @mention message in the same channel where the offending message
was posted.

Success Again! Running Your Second Discord Bot, the Content Moderator

Now let's run our second JavaScript Discord bot. After executing the app,
be sure to return back to your Discord server and type a message in any
channel that contains the offending word. Figure 6-16 shows the bot
in action.

Figure 6-16. *This Bot Has a Strict Rule About Discussing "Puppies"; However, Discussing "Kittens" Is Perfectly Fine*

Conclusion

We just went through all the steps necessary to create two functioning Discord bots in JavaScript. For those who are unfamiliar with the process of creating a Discord server, we showed the process on how to set up a server to manage our community.

As you can see, we took a much different approach compared to our Slack bot that we did in Chapter 4! The Slack bot that we created was pretty much focused on user productivity within the workplace. The two Discord bots, on the other hand, are truly focused on community management. We have everything in place for these bots to be artificially intelligent with the help of OpenAI's APIs. This is all accomplished in the final two chapters.

Exercises Left for the Reader

In the next chapters, we're going to make our "dumb" bots to be intelligent, but there's at least one thing we can do right now. Rather than using the command line to report status messages, it's better for the bots to have their own channel that's exclusively used for status reports. This way, when the bot starts up, shuts down, or has anything important to inform the administrators, it's all logged and recorded in a central location.

CHAPTER 7

Adding Intelligence to Our Discord Bots, Part 1: Improving Our Q&A Bot

At this point, we have all the structure in place to make both our Discord bots that we created in the previous chapter to be fully functional and artificially intelligent. In these final two chapters of this book, we're going to follow all the steps necessary in order to make both bots to be artificially intelligent. In this chapter, we'll get started with our Tech Support Bot. Below are the two major changes that we're going to make:

- Improve our script that calls the OpenAI APIs and make a class that can be instantiated by the Discord bot. This way, the Discord bot class can ask questions about specific information that we provide to it. This class will be used for Q&A purposes in this chapter but will be used in the final chapter of the book as well.

© Bruce Hopkins Jr., Bruce Hopkins Sr. 2025
B. Hopkins Jr. and B. Hopkins Sr., *Creating ChatGPT Apps with JavaScript*,
https://doi.org/10.1007/979-8-8688-1221-7_7

- Modify our Tech Support Discord bot so that it can load an external text file that contains frequently asked questions with the answers. This script will then provide the contents of the text file to the ChatGPTClient class who is responsible for creating the prompt and of course invoking ChatGPT.

Making Our Tech Support Bot More Intelligent

Listing 7-1 contains the full contents of the frequently asked questions that the fictional customer support team has created based upon support tickets from users of the newly launched mobile banking application.

Listing 7-1. FAQ.txt

```
1. What is the Crooks Bank Mobile App?
The Crooks Bank Mobile App is a cutting-edge mobile banking app
that allows you to manage your finances, make transactions, and
access a wide range of banking services conveniently from your
mobile device.

2. How can I download the Crooks Bank Mobile App?
You can download the Crooks Bank Mobile App from the App
Store for iOS devices and Google Play for Android devices.
Simply search for the "Crooks Bank Mobile App" and click the
"Install" button.

3. Is the Crooks Bank Mobile App safe and secure?
Yes, the Crooks Bank Mobile App prioritizes your security.
We use state-of-the-art encryption and security protocols to
protect your data and transactions. Your information is safe
with us.
```

4. What features does the Crooks Bank Mobile App offer?
 The Crooks Bank Mobile App provides a variety of features, including:

- Account Management: View account balances, transaction history, and more.
- Transfer Funds: Easily transfer money between your accounts or to other bank accounts.
- Bill Payments: Pay bills and manage recurring payments.
- Deposit Checks: Snap photos of checks for remote deposit.
- ATM Locator: Find nearby ATMs and branches.
- Notifications: Receive alerts for account activity and important updates.

5. Can I link external accounts to the Crooks Bank Mobile App?
Yes, the Crooks Bank Mobile App supports linking external accounts from other financial institutions. You can monitor and manage your accounts from different banks in one place.

6. How can I reset my password if I forget it?
If you forget your password, simply click the "Forgot Password" option on the login screen. You'll receive instructions on how to reset your password.

7. What are the fees associated with the Crooks Bank Mobile App?
The Crooks Bank Mobile App aims to be transparent with its fees. You can find information on account fees, transaction charges, and other costs in the "Fees" section within the app or on our website.

8. Can I get customer support through the Crooks Bank Mobile App?
Absolutely! We offer customer support through our in-app messaging feature. You can also find our customer service contact information on our website.

9. Is the Crooks Bank Mobile App available for business accounts?
The Crooks Bank Mobile App primarily caters to personal banking needs. However, we have plans to introduce business banking services in the future.

10. How can I provide feedback or suggestions for the Crooks Bank Mobile App?
We welcome your feedback! You can submit suggestions and feedback through the "Contact Us" section in the app or on our website.

As you can see in the Frequently Asked Questions text file in Listing 7-1, there's no magic involved here. It's simply a list of questions and the answers. Now, let's see the modified Tech Support Discord bot. This is represented in Listing 7-2.

Listing 7-2. Our Smarter Tech Support Discord Bot

```
// Require the necessary discord.js classes
const { Client, Events, GatewayIntentBits } =
require("discord.js");
const { ChatGPTClient } = require("./chatGPTClient");
const fs = require("node:fs");
require("dotenv").config();

const systemMessage =
   "You are a virtual assistant that provides support for the
Crooks Bank banking app.";
const faqContents = fs.readFileSync("./FAQ.txt", "utf8");
const chatGPTClient = new ChatGPTClient(systemMessage,
faqContents);
```

```javascript
// Configuration variables
const CHANNEL_NAME = "q-and-a";
const CUSTOM_STATUS = "Ready to answer your questions";

// Create a new Discord client instance
const discordClient = new Client({
  intents: [
    GatewayIntentBits.MessageContent,
    GatewayIntentBits.GuildMessages,
    GatewayIntentBits.Guilds,
  ],
});

discordClient.once(Events.ClientReady, (readyClient) => {
  console.log(`Ready! Logged in as ${readyClient.user.tag}`);
  // Set the custom status
  discordClient.user.setActivity(CUSTOM_STATUS);
});

discordClient.on(Events.MessageCreate, async (message) => {
  if (discordClient.user.username === message.author.
  username) return;
  if (message.channel.name != CHANNEL_NAME) return;

  console.log("User is:", message.author.globalName);
  console.log("Message is:", message.content);

  await message.channel.sendTyping();
  const chatGPTResponse = await chatGPTClient.
  sendMessageFromDiscord(
    message.content
  );
```

```
const reply = `${mention(message.author)}
${chatGPTResponse}`;
await message.channel.send(reply);
});

function mention(author) {
  return `<@${author.id}>`;
}

// Log in to Discord with your client's token
discordClient.login(process.env.DISCORD_BOT_API_TOKEN);
```

Important Changes to Note from the Previous Version of the Tech Support Bot

Let's briefly analyze our updated Tech Support Bot and discuss the changes that were made. As you can see, we're doing a few things at once.

First of all, this script will function as a client to both Discord and ChatGPT, so having a single constant named "client" will be somewhat confusing. Therefore, the client that will be used for any AI operations with ChatGPT is a constant named chatGPTClient:

```
const systemMessage =
  "You are a virtual assistant that provides support for the
  Crooks Bank banking app.";
const faqContents = fs.readFileSync("./FAQ.txt", "utf8");
const chatGPTClient = new ChatGPTClient(systemMessage,
faqContents);
```

Remember from the previous chapters in the book that you can dramatically set the tone of the conversation with ChatGPT by providing a specific message to the system itself in your prompt. Therefore, we made a constant to hold the system message. Additionally, we defined a constant that holds the contents of the frequently asked questions file. With the system message and the contents of the FAQ defined, we're able to instantiate our ChatGPTClient class (more details about that later).

The whole purpose of this bot is to send any message from a Discord user to ChatGPT and display the response. Therefore, let's look at the changes made to client.on(), which has been renamed to discordClient.on().

Updates to the Newly Named Function, discordClient.on()

The discordClient.on() function is asynchronously called every time a message is posted into the discord server. For obvious performance reasons, the code needed to instantiate the chatGPTClient class (which also includes the process of loading the contents from the FAQ.txt file) is not in this function. We already performed those steps earlier in this script seeing that they only need to be done once.

When a message is received into the channel that were observing, be sure to notice the following lines of code:

```
  await message.channel.sendTyping();
  const chatGPTResponse = await chatGPTClient.
  sendMessageFromDiscord(
    message.content
  );

  const reply = `${mention(message.author)}
  ${chatGPTResponse}`;
  await message.channel.send(reply);
});
```

Here, we provide a nice user experience and show the user that the bot is "typing," while the user's question is actually being sent to ChatGPT. When the response comes back, we provide the reply back to the user.

Now let's take a look at our helper class that handles all of our ChatGPT capabilities: chatGPTClient.js.

Analyzing Our ChatGPT Client, chatGPTClient.js

So, we have our own class called chatGPTClient.js, which is very similar to ones we've used before. The complete source for chatGPTClient.js is shown in Listing 7-3.

Listing 7-3. chatGPTClient.js

```
const { OpenAI } = require("openai");
require("dotenv").config();

class ChatGPTClient {
  constructor(systemMessage, initialInstructionsToChatGPT) {
    this.systemMessage = systemMessage;
    this.initialInstructionsToChatGPT =
    initialInstructionsToChatGPT;
    this.client = new OpenAI({
      apiKey: process.env["OPENAI_API_KEY"],
    });
  }

  async sendMessageFromDiscord(userMessage) {
    const chatCompletion = await this.client.chat.completions.
    create({
```

```
    messages: [
      {
        role: "system",
        content: this.systemMessage,
      },
      {
        role: "user",
        content: this.initialInstructionsToChatGPT,
      },
      {
        role: "user",
        content: userMessage,
      },
    ],
    model: "gpt-4",
    temperature: 0.85,
    top_p: 1,
    max_tokens: 1921,
    frequency_penalty: 0,
    presence_penalty: 0,
  });
  const result = chatCompletion.choices[0].message.content;
  return result;
  }
}

module.exports = { ChatGPTClient };
```

One of the most important things to note is that in the constructor, we are sending the full String of the contents of the frequently asked questions as well as the message that we're going to be providing to the system itself.

This way, after we have constructed the ChatGPTClient class, we can reuse the object already constructed in order to ask the individual questions from our users.

Every time a question has been posted on our Discord channel, our bot will call sendMessageFromDiscord() from chatGPTClient.js. In this method, we will perform all of the usual things necessary in order to invoke ChatGPT programmatically.

Running Our Intelligent Q&A Bot

Now let's run our new and improved Q&A Discord bot. After executing the app, be sure to return back to your Discord server and start asking questions. Figure 7-1 shows the bot in action.

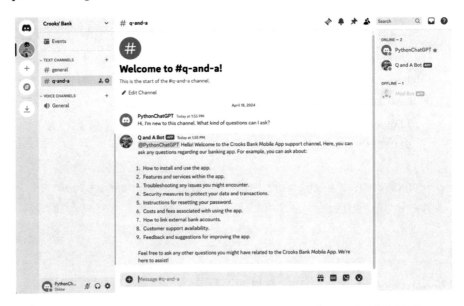

Figure 7-1. *Having a Discussion with Our Intelligent DISCORD Bot for Q&A*

Listing 7-4 shows the conversation between us and the Discord Bot.

Listing 7-4. Our First Conversation with the Intelligent Q&A Discord Bot

Me: Hi, I'm new to this channel. What kind of questions can I ask?

Q and A Bot: Hello! Welcome to the Crooks Bank Mobile App support channel. Here, you can ask any questions regarding our banking app. For example, you can ask about:

1. How to install and use the app.

2. Features and services within the app.

3. Troubleshooting any issues you might encounter.

4. Security measures to protect your data and transactions.

5. Instructions for resetting your password.

6. Costs and fees associated with using the app.

7. How to link external bank accounts.

8. Customer support availability.

9. Feedback and suggestions for improving the app.

Feel free to ask any other questions you might have related to the Crooks Bank Mobile App. We're here to assist!

Me: I have an old Blackberry phone, is the app supported on my device?

Q and A Bot: I'm sorry for the inconvenience, but at the moment, the Crooks Bank Mobile App is currently only available for iOS and Android devices. It is not supported on Blackberry or any other operating systems. You may still manage your bank accounts by accessing our website through your phone's browser.

Me: I'm an iPhone user. Can I sign into the app with face or touch ID?

Q and A Bot: Sure, here's how you can set up the Crooks Bank Mobile App on your iPhone:

1. Open the App Store on your iPhone.
2. In the search bar at the top, type in "Crooks Bank Mobile App" and tap "Search".
3. Once you can see the app in the search results, simply tap on the "Get" button to download it.
4. After the app downloads, tap "Open".
5. You'll have to agree to our Terms and Conditions upon the first launch.
6. If you're an existing Crooks Bank member, you can log in using your online banking user ID and password. If you're a new member, you'll need to register for an account.
7. Once you're logged in, you can set up Touch ID or Face ID for quicker, secure login in the future.
8. Now you can start using your Crooks Bank Mobile App to manage your finances, pay bills, make transactions, and more!

Please make sure you update the app regularly to access new features and improvements. If you have any challenges during setup, please reach out to us through the app's support feature or call our customer service.

We Have a Monumental Achievement… with One Slight Flaw

OK, if you step back and examine what we have achieved so far, you should realize that we're looking at what is nothing short of a monumental achievement. We have the following:

- A system made up of a few scripts that allows users to type in questions and get answers about how to use our mobile application.

- Using a simple text file, we can teach our bot how to answer the questions from our users. This can be edited by anyone in the company and can be used as a knowledge base to help improve the intelligence of the bot day by day. This is amazing stuff.

- The system allows customers to type their questions using natural language, and the bot provides an intelligent answer back to them. Guess what? Customers don't like reading FAQs – especially really long ones. However, using this system, they don't need to! All they have to do is ask the question that is relevant to them.

So, with all this that we have accomplished, there's one GIGANTIC flaw that we can't ignore. In Listing 7-4, the bot said to the user:

```
Once you're logged in, you can set up Touch ID or Face ID for
quicker, secure login in the future.
```

No, no, no! Bad bot! In case you didn't read the frequently asked questions file completely, please allow me to explain what went wrong here:

1. The FAQ.txt file in Listing 7-1 clearly states that the Crooks Bank mobile app is a mobile app. Currently, Touch ID can only be used on Apple desktop and laptop computers. So this doesn't even make sense.

2. The FAQ.txt file has no mention of Face ID for authentication to the mobile app at all.

So unfortunately, ChatGPT is making up things that are simply not true and is assuming that certain features exist that are not present. So, for the purposes of true tech support, this is absolutely unacceptable.

So, how do we solve this? Think about how you could solve this problem for a second before reading the next section.

Update the System Message to ChatGPT and Let's Try Again

Have you come up with a solution yet? One way to resolve this issue is to update the System message. Refer to the following line in Listing 7-2 above:

```
const systemMessage =
  "You are a virtual assistant that provides support for the
Crooks Bank banking app.";
```

Remember that the System Message indicates to ChatGPT what it's role is in the chat conversation. Right now it is told to be a helpful assistant, and therefore it has taken the liberty in order to guess that certain features exist within the mobile application. Now, let's ensure that ChatGPT does not provide any assumptions. Update the System Message to be as shown below:

```
const systemMessage = "You are a virtual assistant that
provides support for the Crooks Bank banking app. You will be
provided Information about the application, and users will ask
```

you questions about the application. Your role is to answer questions explicitly from the training information. If you were not given an answer to a question, then provide an apologetic message to the user explaining that you do not know the answer.";

And that's it. The FAQ.txt file remains exactly the same as before, and all we needed to do is to update the System Message to let ChatGPT know it's role in the conversation. Listing 7-5 has the new conversation between us and the Discord bot.

Listing 7-5. Our Second and Better Conversation with the Intelligent Q&A Discord Bot

Me: How are you today?

Q and A Bot: As a virtual assistant, I don't have feelings or emotions, but I'm here and ready to assist you. How may I help you with the Crooks Bank Mobile App today?

Me: I have an old Blackberry phone, is the app supported on my device?

Q and A Bot: I'm sorry, but from the information provided, the Crooks Bank Mobile App can only be downloaded from the App Store for iOS devices and Google Play for Android devices. BlackBerry devices are not mentioned, therefore I cannot confirm that it would be compatible.

Me: So, if I use an iPhone, how do I setup the app?

Q and A Bot: To set up the Crooks Bank Mobile App on your iPhone, you can download it from the App Store. Simply search for "Crooks Bank Mobile App" and click the "Install" button. After the installation is finished, open the app and follow the prompts to set up your account. If you already have an account, use your login information to access your account through the app.

Now that's a lot better! Our Tech Support bot is "sticking to the script" and is not allowed to makeup or assume anything.

Conclusion

In this chapter, we've accomplished a lot! We have a fully functioning Discord bot that can be trained by anyone without any experience in AI, NLP, or Machine Learning using a simple text file. We learned that a "helpful assistant" may at times become TOO HELPFUL and assume facts that are not true. However, we also reiterated the concept and the value of the System Message, which is an important part of Prompt Engineering.

Now that we have made our Q&A Discord bot to be intelligent, now let's find out how to make out Content Moderator bot to be intelligent as well!

CHAPTER 8

Adding Intelligence to Our Discord Bots, Part 2: Improving Our Moderator Bot

In this chapter, we're going to take the steps necessary in order to make our Content Moderator Discord bot artificially intelligent. Here's the kind of changes that we're going to make.

First of all, we're going to create a new script to invoke one of the **Moderations** models. The Moderations models are a special category of models that allow us to be aware when any textual content fits any of the following categories:

- Hate

- Hate/threatening

- Harassment

- Harassment/threatening

- Self-harm

- Self-harm/intent

© Bruce Hopkins Jr., Bruce Hopkins Sr. 2025
B. Hopkins Jr. and B. Hopkins Sr., *Creating ChatGPT Apps with JavaScript*,
https://doi.org/10.1007/979-8-8688-1221-7_8

- Self-harm/instructions

- Sexual

- Sexual/minors

- Violence

- Violence/graphic

Next, we're going to reuse our chatGPTClient.js script from the previous chapter. In Chapter 7, it was used to invoke a Chat model using the client.chat.completions.create() method for Q&A purposes from our users. In this chapter, it will be used to invoke a Chat model again, but this time for moderation purposes.

Of course, we're going to update our chatGPTClient.js script so that it can invoke a Moderation model.

And finally, we're going to modify our Content Moderator Discord bot so that it can invoke both a Chat and Moderation model in chatGPTClient. js. If either models indicate that the content typed in the Discord channel is objectionable, then delete the message from that Discord channel. Remember, this bot watches all content in all channels of the Discord server!

Note   Now, it this point, you may be asking yourself, if the Moderation models already know how to flag any harmful content, then why do we need to use any of the Chat models as well? Good question.

Yes, the Moderation models will allow us to know about harmful content, but it **DOES NOT** inform us about any other types of unwanted content for our scenario, such as when unscrupulous

individuals try to lure our users into a scam. Remember, this is a
Discord server for a banking app, so scammers would definitely love
to target all the members of this Discord server since it's a central
location full of bank users!

Therefore, in this final chapter, we're going to invoke both Chat and
Moderation models in chatGPTClient.js.

Using OpenAI.moderations.create() to Invoke a Moderation Model

Any of the Moderation models allows developers to submit a String of text
and to subsequently know if it's violent, hateful, threatening, or contains
any form of harassment.

Table 8-1 describes the format of the parameters necessary to call the
body for the OpenAI.moderations.create() method. The method is very
simple to use, since only one parameter is required to properly invoke the
service.

Create Moderation (JSON)

Table 8-1. *The Request Body for the Moderation Method*

Field	Type	Required?	Description
input	String or Array	Required	The text that needs to be classified
model	String default: "omni-moderation-latest"	Optional	There are multiple content moderation models available for use, for example: • "omni-moderation-latest" • "text-moderation-stable" • "text-moderation-latest" By default, this is set to "omni-moderation-latest." It will be automatically upgraded over time, which ensures you're always using the most accurate model. If you decide to use any of the text based moderation models, then you are only able to submit text to be evaluated. The omni moderation models, however, are able to evaluate content as text and images. Therefore choose the model that works best for your use case.

Handling the JSON Response

After successfully invoking a Moderation model, the API will provide a JSON response with the structure shown in Table 8-2.

Moderation (JSON)

Table 8-2. *The Structure of the Moderation JSON Object*

Field	Type	Description
id	String	A unique identifier for the moderation request
model	String	The model used to perform the moderation request
results	Array	A list of moderation objects
↳ flagged	Boolean	Flags if the content violates OpenAI's usage policies
↳ categories	Array	A list of the categories and whether they're being flagged or not
↳↳ hate	Boolean	This indicates whether or not the text given expresses, incites, or promotes hate based on race, gender, religion, ethnicity, nationality, disability status, sexual orientation, or caste
↳↳ hate/ threatening	Boolean	This indicates whether or not the text given contains hateful content that also threatens violence or serious harm toward the targeted group based on biases expressed above
↳↳ harassment	Boolean	This indicates whether or not the text given contains content that expresses, incites, or promotes harassing language toward any target
↳↳ harassment/ threatening	Boolean	This indicates whether or not the text given contains harassment content that also threatens violence or serious harm toward any target.
↳↳ self-harm	Boolean	This indicates whether or not the text given contains content that promotes, encourages, or depicts acts of self-harm, for example, suicide, cutting, and eating disorders.

(continued)

Table 8-2. (*continued*)

Field	Type	Description
↳↳ self-harm/ intent	Boolean	This indicates whether or not the text given contains content in which the speaker expresses that they are engaging or intend to engage in acts of self-harm, such as suicide, cutting, and eating disorders.
↳↳ self-harm/ instructions	Boolean	This indicates whether or not the text given contains content that encourages the performing acts of self-harm, such as suicide, cutting, and eating disorders. This includes content that gives instructions or advice on how to commit such acts
↳↳ sexual	Boolean	This indicates whether or not the text given contains content meant to arouse sexual excitement, such as the description of sexual activity. This includes content that promotes sexual services; however, this ***excludes*** topics such as sex education and wellness.
↳↳ sexual/ minors	Boolean	This indicates whether or not the text given contains content that includes an individual under the age of 18
↳↳ violence	Boolean	This indicates whether or not the text given contains content depicting death, violence, or physical injury
↳↳ violence/ graphic	Boolean	This indicates whether or not the text given contains content depicting death, violence, or physical injury in graphic detail.

(*continued*)

Table 8-2. (*continued*)

Field	Type	Description
↳ category_ scores	Array	A list of the categories along with the scores given by the model
↳↳ hate	Number	Score for the category "hate"
↳↳ hate/ threatening	Number	Score for the category "hate/threatening"
↳↳ harassment	Number	Score for the category "harassment"
↳↳ harassment/ threatening	Number	Score for the category "harassment/threatening"
↳↳ self-harm	Number	Score for the category "self-harm"
↳↳ self-harm/ intent	Number	Score for the category "self-harm/intent"
↳↳ self-harm/ instructions	Number	Score for the category "self-harm/instructions"
↳↳ sexual	Number	Score for the category "sexual"
↳↳ violence	Number	Score for the category "violence"
↳↳ violence/ graphic	Number	Score for the category "violence/graphic"

The listing below is an example of the JSON response after invoking a Moderation model. Table 8-2 looks a little complex, but as you can see, if any of the categories is labeled as "true," then the **results.flagged** node is labeled as "true."

Take a look at Listing 8-1 for a practical example of the
Moderation object.

Listing 8-1. The Moderation Object Response

```
{
  "id": "modr-XXXXX",
  "model": "text-moderation-005",
  "results": [
    {
    "flagged": true,
    "categories": {
      "sexual": false,
      "hate": false,
      "harassment": false,
      "self-harm": false,
      "sexual/minors": false,
      "hate/threatening": false,
      "violence/graphic": false,
      "self-harm/intent": false,
      "self-harm/instructions": false,
      "harassment/threatening": true,
      "violence": true,
    },
    "category_scores": {
      "sexual": 1.2282071e-06,
      "hate": 0.010696256,
      "harassment": 0.29842457,
```

```
        "self-harm": 1.5236925e-08,
        "sexual/minors": 5.7246268e-08,
        "hate/threatening": 0.0060676364,
        "violence/graphic": 4.435014e-06,
        "self-harm/intent": 8.098441e-10,
        "self-harm/instructions": 2.8498655e-11,
        "harassment/threatening": 0.63055265,
        "violence": 0.99011886,
      }
    }
  ]
}
```

Creating Our Client for Content Moderation

Listing 8-2 is our updated chatGPTClient.js script that's been updated from the previous chapter to allow us to use it for invoking both a Chat model and a Moderation model. Take a look at it, and then we'll discuss the important parts afterward.

Listing 8-2. The Updated chatgptclient.js

```
const { OpenAI } = require("openai");
require("dotenv").config();

class ChatGPTClient {
  constructor(systemMessage, initialInstructionsToChatGPT) {
    this.systemMessage = systemMessage;
    this.initialInstructionsToChatGPT =
    initialInstructionsToChatGPT;
```

```
    this.client = new OpenAI({
      apiKey: process.env["OPENAI_API_KEY"],
    });
  }

  async sendMessageFromDiscord(userMessage) {
    const chatCompletion = await this.client.chat.completions.
    create({
      messages: [
        {
          role: "system",
          content: this.systemMessage,
        },
        {
          role: "user",
          content: this.initialInstructionsToChatGPT,
        },
        {
          role: "user",
          content: userMessage,
        },
      ],
      model: "gpt-4",
      temperature: 0.85,
      top_p: 1,
      max_tokens: 1000,
      frequency_penalty: 0,
      presence_penalty: 0,
    });
    const result = chatCompletion.choices[0].message.content;
    return result;
  }
```

```
  async isFlagged(message) {
    const response = await this.client.moderations.create({
      input: message,
    });
    return response.results[0].flagged;
  }
}

module.exports = { ChatGPTClient };
```

If you recall how this script worked from the previous chapter, we defined a class with a constructor for the operations that should only be done once, namely, specifying the system message and the initial instruction to ChatGPT. None of this has changed from the previous chapter.

The same thing applies to the sendMessageFromDiscord() function. We use this to invoke the Chat model of our choice using the text of what was typed in the Discord channel. As you'll see later in this chapter, the initial instructions will be different from the previous chapter, but the code still works the same.

However, let's analyze the following asynchronous function that was added to the script:

```
  async isFlagged(message) {
    const response = await this.client.moderations.create({
      input: message,
    });
    return response.results[0].flagged;
  }
```

As you can see, using these few lines of code, this is how we are able to invoke a Moderations model by calling OpenAI.moderations.create() and determine if the content has been flagged as being inappropriate.

Making Our Content Moderator Bot More Intelligent

Now that we have an improved chatGPTClient.js script that is capable of moderating content using both a Chat and a Moderation model, let's examine the changes made to our Discord Bot for Content Moderation.

Listing 8-3 is the full source code for our intelligent Discord Moderator Bot.

Listing 8-3. Our Improved Content Moderator Bot

```
// Require the necessary discord.js classes
const { Client, Events, GatewayIntentBits } =
require("discord.js");
const { ChatGPTClient } = require("./chatGPTClient");
const fs = require("node:fs");
require("dotenv").config();

const systemMessage = `
You are the automated moderator assistant for a Discord server.
Review each message for the following rule violations:
1. Sensitive information
2. Abuse
3. Inappropriate comments
4. Spam, for example; a message in all capital letters, the
same phrase or word being repeated over and over, more than 3
exclamation marks or question marks.
5. Advertisement
6. External links
7. Political messages or debate
8. Religious messages or debate
```

If any of these violations are detected, respond with "FLAG"
(in uppercase without quotation marks). If the message adheres
to the rules, respond with "SAFE" (in uppercase without
quotation marks).

```
`;
const instructions = "Analyze the following message for rule
violations:";
const chatGPTClient = new ChatGPTClient(systemMessage,
instructions);

// Create a new client instance
const discordClient = new Client({
  intents: [
    GatewayIntentBits.MessageContent,
    GatewayIntentBits.GuildMessages,
    GatewayIntentBits.Guilds,
  ],
});

discordClient.once(Events.ClientReady, (readyClient) => {
  console.log(`Ready! Logged in as ${readyClient.user.tag}`);
});

discordClient.on(Events.MessageCreate, async (message) => {
  if (discordClient.user.username === message.author.
  username) return;

  console.log("User is:", message.author.globalName);
  console.log("Message is:", message.content);

  const chatGPTResponse = await chatGPTClient.
  sendMessageFromDiscord(
    message.content
  );
```

```
const isFlagged = await chatGPTClient.isFlagged(message.
content);

if (chatGPTResponse === "FLAG" || isFlagged) {
  if (!(await message.delete())) {
    console.log("Failed to delete message");
  } else {
    const authorMention = `${mention(message.author)}`;
    const reply = `${authorMention} This comment was deemed
    inappropriate for this channel.\nIf you believe this
    to be in error, please contact one of the human server
    moderators.`;
    await message.channel.send(reply);
  }
}
});

function mention(author) {
  return `<@${author.id}>`;
}

// Log in to Discord with your client's token
discordClient.login(process.env.DISCORD_BOT_API_TOKEN);
```

Important Changes to Note from the Previous Version of the Content Moderator Bot

Let's briefly take a look at Content Moderator Discord Bot from Listing 8-3 and discuss the changes that were made. The code snippet below contains a portion of the class definition section.

```
const systemMessage = `
You are the automated moderator assistant for a Discord server.
Review each message for the following rule violations:
1. Sensitive information
2. Abuse
3. Inappropriate comments
4. Spam, for example; a message in all capital letters, the
same phrase or word being repeated over and over, more than 3
exclamation marks or question marks.
5. Advertisement
6. External links
7. Political messages or debate
8. Religious messages or debate

If any of these violations are detected, respond with "FLAG"
(in uppercase without quotation marks). If the message adheres
to the rules, respond with "SAFE" (in uppercase without
quotation marks).
`;
const instructions = "Analyze the following message for rule
violations:";
const chatGPTClient = new ChatGPTClient(systemMessage,
instructions);
```

So, as we stated previously in this book, proper prompt engineering requires you to use multiple parameters, including the "system message" to the system itself. Here, we're telling the Chat model all the types of information that we don't want posted in our Discord server.

We hope you can understand the reason why our Discord Moderator Bot needs to use both a Chat model as well as a Moderation model from OpenAI. The Moderation models work fine "out of the box" for basic

content moderation; however, since our use case is for a bank, we want
to take extra precautions in order to prevent our customers from being
targeted by unscrupulous individuals through our Discord server.

Updates to the discordClient.on() Function

After a message is received in any channel of the Discord server, the
discordClient.on() function is invoked. Here's the most important change
to be aware of:

```
discordClient.on(Events.MessageCreate, async (message) => {

  ...

  const chatGPTResponse = await chatGPTClient.
  sendMessageFromDiscord(
    message.content
  );
  const isFlagged = await chatGPTClient.isFlagged(message.
  content);

  if (chatGPTResponse === "FLAG" || isFlagged) {
    if (!(await message.delete())) {
      console.log("Failed to delete message");
    } else {
      const authorMention = `${mention(message.author)}`;
      const reply = `${authorMention} This comment was deemed
      inappropriate for this channel.\nIf you believe this
      to be in error, please contact one of the human server
      moderators.`;
      await message.channel.send(reply);
    }
  }
});
```

Here, we take each message that was posted in the Discord server and check it with both Chat and Moderation models. If either model informs us that the message is flagged, then we delete the message in the channel and inform the user that their message violated the rules.

Now that our Content Moderator Discord bot is intelligent, let's give it a try!

Running Our Intelligent Content Moderator Bot

Now let's run our new and improved Content Moderator Discord bot. After executing the app, be sure to return back to your Discord server and start asking questions. Figure 8-1 shows the bot in action.

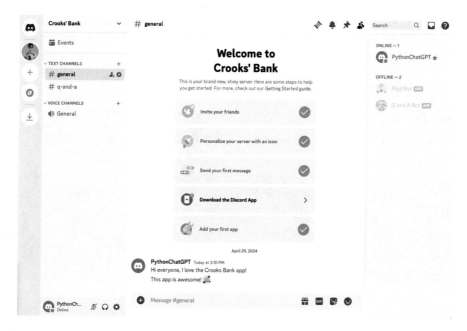

Figure 8-1. *Having a Discussion with Our Intelligent DISCORD Content Moderator Bot*

Listing 8-4 shows a conversation between us and the Discord Bot in order to test to see what it can do.

Listing 8-4. Our Offensive Conversation with the Intelligent Moderator Discord Bot

Me: Hi everyone, I love the Crooks Bank app!

Me: This app is awesome! 😵

Me: Come to my website! http://www.google.com

Content Mod Bot: @JSChatGPT This comment was deemed inappropriate for this channel. If you believe this to be in error, please contact one of the human server moderators.

Me: I'm sorry for breaking the rules. I'm a different person now

Me: But I have some sad news for you

Me: I want to 💀 everyone

Content Mod Bot: @JSChatGPT This comment was deemed inappropriate for this channel. If you believe this to be in error, please contact one of the human server moderators.

In both cases when unwanted content was posted in any channel of the Discord server, not only was the offending user called out, but the bad message was deleted. Good bot!

Did you notice that the Moderation and Chat models are able to read emojis as well?

Conclusion

In this chapter, we created a fully functioning content moderator for our entire Discord server! We leveraged both the Moderation and Chat models from OpenAI to create a custom content moderator that not only flags unsafe content like hateful and threatening messages but also prevents the users of the Discord server to be subject to unwanted solicitations.

Exercises Left for the Reader

Although we accomplished a lot in this chapter (as well as in this book!), there's still one more thing that we can do to improve the code.

For example, the individual Discord bots that we created are aware to not respond to messages that they send themselves. However, the bots are not yet aware that they shouldn't respond to messages sent by **OTHER BOTS**.

This means that if you run both bots at the same time, and someone posts something bad in the "q-and-a" channel, then the Content Moderator will (of course) delete the message and inform everyone that the message was deleted. However, since the Tech Support Bot doesn't know that it shouldn't respond to other bots, it will try to create a response. Of course, bots should not talk to other bots.

Index

© Bruce Hopkins Jr., Bruce Hopkins Sr. 2025
B. Hopkins Jr. and B. Hopkins Sr., *Creating ChatGPT Apps with JavaScript*,
https://doi.org/10.1007/979-8-8688-1221-7

219

F

FFmpeg, 133, 135, 151
ffmpeg.ffprobe() function, 135

G

Generative AI models, 121
Google Maps
    account setup, 53
    homepage, 52
    JavaScript API, 56, 57
    keys and credentials, 58
    navigate API, 54, 55

H

Human intelligence, 132

I

Investigative journalism, 138

J, K

JavaScript
    browser compatibility, 86
    client-side processing, 86
    community/resources, 86
    evolving, 86
    frameworks, 86
    interactivity, 85
    JSON, 86
    libraries, 86
    real-time feedback, 86
    versatility, 86
JavaScript developers
    Module pattern, 4
    Observer pattern, 4
    Singleton pattern, 5
JavaScript Object Notation
    (JSON), 86
JSON, *see* JavaScript Object
    Notation (JSON)

L

Language models, 3

M

Memory-related anomalies, 102
models.list() function, 34
Moderation models
    asynchronous function, 209
    chatgptclient.js, 207
    create, 202
    definition, 199
    JSON object, 203
    JSON response, 202
    object response, 206
Module pattern, 4

N

Natural Language
    Processing (NLP), 6
Natural Language
    Understanding (NLU), 6

Printed in the United States
by Baker & Taylor Publisher Services